BEYOND

— THE —

NAME

**Preserving Love, Legacy and Leadership
in Your Family Business**

Brent Patmos

BRENT PATMOS

Printed in the United States of America
First Printing, 2016

Library of Congress: 2016935048
ISBN Hardbound: 978-0-9969659-0-3
ISBN ePub: 978-0-9969659-1-0
ISBN Mobi: 978-0-9969659-3-4

Cover design: Angelina Briggs, studioA, www.artbystudioa.com
Cover photo: Allen W. Royce, www.bestcapturedmoments.com
Interior layout: Fusion Creative Works, www.fusioncw.com
Primary editor: Stacy Ennis, www.stacyennis.com

Perpetual Development
3303 S. Lindsay Rd., #119
Gilbert, AZ 85297

www.perpetualdevelopment.com
www.brentpatmos.com

DEDICATION

TO NEIL

for your leadership, vision, commitment and
impact on generations of families.

TO HARRY

for your leadership and modeling, both at
work and with your family.

TO THE MEMORY OF MY GRANDPARENTS

for the impact they've had on our family.

CONTENTS

Introduction

In 1986, when I was twenty-two years old, my parents gave me a complete original set of University of Michigan china. This wasn't disposable tableware. This was china—the real, the original, the non-disposable.

The china was contained in a set of simple brown moving boxes. Each box was labeled, and after opening the top flap of one of the boxes, I could see that each piece was wrapped individually and thoroughly in newspaper. Each dish had been meticulously packed in the boxes in order to pass on the set safely with love and care.

Each "plate," as I casually referred to all the pieces, had images of university buildings and landmarks. The background was white, with the images and foreground in what is best referred to as china blue. The plates were commanding and yet possessed a delicate nature.

When I received that set of china, there were no conditions and no requirements. There was just the awareness that the dishes had belonged to my grandparents and had been in the family for generations, and now my parents were passing them on to me. Since there were no specific instructions from them, they must have assumed I knew what they wanted me to do with them. Or maybe they thought that since the set had been passed among previous generations, I would automatically know the importance of preserving this china for future generations of our family. Wrong. What did I do instead?

I sold it.

Ypsilanti, Michigan, where I was living at the time, is 8.1 miles from Ann Arbor, the home of the University of Michigan. I was a recent college graduate just starting my career and making $240 gross each week. I was more concerned about money than I was about plates. I wasn't thinking about the fact that my parents had given me a complete and original set of china that was no longer made.

As quickly as I had taken possession of the set, I determined that these plates were taking up valuable space. They had no real emotional connection for me. There certainly was not the awareness needed to preserve the legacy of the china and the love with which it was passed to me.

I placed a classified ad that was printed on the same kind of newsprint the china was wrapped in. I sold the dishes to someone who quickly recognized what a complete set of original U of M china, not replicas, was worth. The total sale price: $750.

Looking back, I recognize that I took possession of the china; what I needed to do instead was take ownership. Then and only then would I have understood the legacy of these timeless pieces based on the family dinner tables they had been set on and the meals they had held.

When I think back on this story, what I could have sold the set for or what it would be worth today isn't what nags at me. It's not about the money. The irritation and frustration I have with myself in not valuing the love and legacy of that dinnerware nag at me like a pulled muscle that won't heal. You learn to live with the discomfort, but it produces a dull ache that always reminds you it's there. You know that nauseous feeling of wanting something back that you've lost or let go of? That's exactly how I feel about our family's University of Michigan china.

The manner in which our family china was passed down is how a lot of family companies are transitioned from one generation to the next. The earlier generation typically assumes the next generation will know what to do with the business and how it should be run. There is often minimal communication and limited instruction.

In the late 1980s, an employer of mine by the name of Fred Meijer shared another important lesson with me about legacy and leadership. Fred, who insisted being called by his first name, shared this lesson out of a love for his business, our customers, and the associates of his company whom he frequently referred to as his extended family. Sitting in a Meijer Thrifty Acres, known today as Meijer, in Taylor, Michigan, over a cup of coffee, Fred took the time to invest in me as a person and a young leader for the company.

"Do you know why every time you walk your parking lot, you should push stray shopping carts into the store?" he asked.

"It's so we always understand the job and role of our baggers, keep our lots clean and are never above any job in the store," I replied.

"That's right," he said. I sat silently and respectfully, waiting for his next words.

"We don't have a janitorial position in our stores, Brent. That's because I expect that every one of us will notice and take care of trash on the floor, spills in an aisle, a cart on the lot or something else that needs attention. None of us should be above doing the job of a fellow associate, and none of us are above doing any job in order to make sure our customers are happy, taken care of and keep shopping in our stores."

Founded in 1934 as a supermarket chain, Meijer is credited with pioneering the modern supercenter concept in 1962. This was the owner and chairman of one of the largest privately held companies in the United States, and he had just advised me to think more critically in his humble, unassuming and yet purposeful way. I knew that in that moment—like so many other instances I later had in my nearly thirteen-year career with the company—I was being practically mentored and taught about leadership all in the same breath. What I didn't understand then but do now is the profound impact such moments would have on the course of my future.

Like Fred, the owners, leaders and family members I work with are deeply committed to the people who make up their companies. They are invested in the leadership and legacy of generations. They not only care, they have a deep and abiding passion and love for preserving and advancing the family company. They know and appreciate the fact that to whom much is given, much is expected.

This book is about maximizing people's potential and, in turn, maximizing a family company's performance and results. Each chapter is written to help preserve and advance the love, legacy and leadership that make the family business an exceptionally unique enterprise. Such companies are the core of opportunity, stability, advancement and growth within our country and around the world, and I get the honor of helping these organizations advance and thrive.

By the way, if you were to visit our home today, we would gladly show and share with you the history of several complete and original sets of "plates," fifty years of Christmas ornaments, family quilts, the Hyde Family Journal, family videos, complete and original first-edition books, family Bibles, and war memorabilia of family members who have served to protect the freedoms of our country.

Legacy is about more than just the "stuff" we pass down. It's about the love those items—and those companies—contain and the leadership we must deliver to maintain the legacy. That's the business of family and the family business.

1

Family Businesses Are Different

"They don't prepare you for that." That's the sentiment I've heard, in varying forms, throughout the years in my work with family-owned businesses.

As a family business owner, they don't prepare you to hand over the company you've spent the better part of your life building and leading. They don't teach you how to choose the right leaders to continue the family legacy. They don't show you how to deal with the sudden death of a family member who is part of the business, or how to fire a relative if that's what needs to be done, or how to work with incoming leaders who have new, fresh ideas that seem counter to everything you've done in the past.

As a new leader in a family business, they don't prepare you for forging your own way, for leading authentically and differently while still honoring the leadership of the past. They don't direct you on how to consistently grow the company and decide which new opportunities to pursue. They don't teach you how to manage the complex family dynamics that undoubtedly complicate matters within the organization. They don't show you how to handle an abrupt generational transition, or how to survive economic hardships, or even how to communicate with others on your leadership team effectively.

Regardless of how successful you are as an owner or leader in a family business, regardless of the ways in which you've proven over the years, decades, even generations that your family business will continue to succeed, there is always, always a level at which you will feel underprepared.

I'll ask a simple question: Who is the "they" who should be preparing you?

In the family business structure, there is often no "they" to step in and prepare you. You have to be the they. You must be intentional about preparing *yourself.*

That is what this book is about. This book is meant to help nudge you, to push you, to even shove you in a direction that causes you to step back, take a look around and determine whether it's time to start being more intentional in the way you lead, grow or transition your organization.

Up until this point, you may have been in survival mode, questioning what's next, simply existing from one moment to the next. It's likely you've tried several different approaches, believing growth would eventually come. You may very well be standing on the doorstep of opportunity, one good strategy away from catapulting your business to the next and greatest level yet. Wherever you find yourself in the business life cycle, I want to help you thrive.

I've had the privilege to serve as a business advisor to some of the top family-owned businesses in the country. These aren't glamorous organizations, ones you'd read about in the media or hear of from your friends; they're some of the most "well-unknown" companies anywhere. Descending from the foremost innovators in our country, these are people who represent the backbone of our nation. They've taken ideas—whether to sell machine parts, operate a retail chain, run a large science lab, sell commercial real estate, or open food manufacturing or processing plants—and they've worked and worked and then worked some more. It's not about the vertical, market or industry. All of the leaders I work with have one thing in common: Their businesses are family owned, led, or managed.

And once they've reached a place of success, they've taken another step. Leaders of these multimillion-dollar companies have asked, "What can we do better? How can we prepare for the future? How can we invest in our people and processes to keep this business thriving for generations to come?"

Will you ask those questions? Will you challenge yourself to become better than good, to become great? Because I'll tell you right now, what separates the companies who thrive into the future isn't luck or chance, and it sometimes isn't even working harder. Often, it's a willingness to be open, to step back, to assess what's really going on and how it can be done better. It's learning the intricate balance of family dynamics, people and processes.

IS IT TIME?

About 35 percent of Fortune 500 companies are family controlled. Family businesses account for 64 percent of US gross domestic product and 62 percent of the country's employment.[1] Clearly, these businesses are key to our economy.

Most family companies believe they will last for generations, but the statistics say otherwise. While 30 percent of family-owned companies will survive into the second generation, only 12 percent will make it to the third generation, and just 3 percent survive into the fourth. On average, family control over the family's core company will remain intact for just over sixty years.[2] And while sixty years is an incredible accomplishment, most of the individuals I work with expect their companies to be around much longer. They see a nearly indefinite future of growth and success well beyond even the fourth or fifth generations.

How can your company outlive those statistics? Purposeful thinking. Intentional planning. Active doing. Effective measuring.

Successful family companies are built by driven individuals with great ideas and the energy to grow their vision into something bigger than themselves. These organizations are led with integrity and passion. The businesses become, in many ways, a part of the family themselves. Employees become more than workers—they become brothers and sisters, aunts and uncles (and sometimes they actually are). The best family-owned companies take on a feel and relationship of their own, a place in the owner's life that is like a different sort of kinship. These businesses are, in some ways, like very complex children.

Unfortunately, here's where the problem arises: Well-meaning owners and leaders don't let their children grow up. Like in parenting, hurdles come up, and leadership guides their child, their business, through each challenge. But when the child is ready to become a full-fledged adult, and it's time to pass the adult child into new hands, leadership resists or denies that it's time.

Time to try new things, transition leadership, and advance thinking. Time to build on the possibilities of the future.

If you are reading this book, my guess is you are not in denial. You are in acceptance. You know that while your business is a success, it's time to push towards something better. There is a greater potential out there that you're not yet reaching. Or you realize that you're not the one to lead the company towards that potential and it's time to transition to new leadership—maybe your son or daughter, niece or nephew, or a non-family member. Perhaps you are a seasoned leader getting ready to take over the company or an up-and-coming leader trying to make sense of the family structure.

> **It's time to push towards something better. There is a greater potential out there that you're not yet reaching.**

Whatever your place in the complex world of the family-owned business, you're starting right where you should.

The most successful family business owners and leaders I've worked with follow four simple steps: think, plan, do, measure. I'll touch on that concept again later, but the key is the active process of all four. You may be tempted to move into autopilot, removing your hands from the steering wheel because it is *just so easy* to let things run the way they're running. But the greatest leaders think actively about the future, planning for how they want to change, to do things differently, to shake up their world in a good way. Then, they do. They make things happen. Finally, they loop around by measuring their progress, assessing where they are and whether they've been successful. Often, they start the cycle once or many times more and think, plan, do and measure all over again.

The first step, before any of this can occur, is thinking: differently, critically and purposefully. That's what I want for you as a leader. That's what I will push you to do throughout this book.

The first key to the process of thinking differently? Be willing to look at your organization objectively. We'll begin by exploring how your family business is different.

WHY FAMILY BUSINESSES ARE DIFFERENT

Every year, a client of mine holds a golf outing for company managers. Around two hundred office and management professionals attend this event each year, which represents about 10 percent of their total workforce. The weekend includes a dinner held in a big event tent, complete with white linen tablecloths and a hearty steak dinner. The event buzzes with excitement and energy, as though old friends are coming together to catch up after years away. Every time I attend, I can't help but feel as though I'm at a big family reunion.

Last year, after warm exchanges and plenty of laughter, everyone took their seats as the human resources (HR) director approached the microphone and began the evening. Every person in the room knew what to expect: the annual call of service.

The HR director asked the attendees to stand. Each of the two hundred people in the room rose to their feet, waiting for what was coming next.

He began, "Anyone who has one year or less of service with the company, please sit." A handful of individuals took their seats.

"Anyone who has under five years of service, please sit." Again, a small number of people sat down. The majority of the room stood standing, slight smiles on their faces.

Imagine, if you will, what would occur at a typical company. Wouldn't maybe a quarter of the room be sitting by then? By the time the HR director got to ten years of service, at least 50 percent of the leaders in a "typical" company gathering would be seated.

Not this company. By the time the HR director reached ten years, still *three-quarters* of the room stood. Seventy-five percent of the leadership!

Fifteen years. Half remained standing.

Twenty years. A third of the room still stood.

He kept going until he reached the longest-serving employee, with fifty-two years of service.

While this may be unusual in many companies, it is not unusual in the family businesses I work with. In fact, it is one of the key differentiators between publicly held and family-owned businesses. More than just words or statements hung on the wall, a commitment to people is at the core of well-run family organizations. They stick around for the long haul. Like the employees at the golf outing, these people continue dedicated service for decades, and that commitment becomes a badge of honor. It is also an obligation.

The leaders and employees in family businesses take success and failure personally. They know what underachievement means to the people in the plant, store or warehouse. If employees are laid off, they feel a sense of responsibility unparalleled in the publicly held world.

Family companies are also different in other ways than just length of service. In the publicly held world, leaders work from a perspective of shareholder returns and quarterly dividends. By the very nature of the business structure, they're required to resolve conflicts quickly by whatever means necessary to produce the end result. Underperforming for one quarter is a concern; underperforming for multiple quarters becomes detrimental to both the people and the organization. That's when budgets are cut, layoffs happen, employees leave for more stable jobs, and drastic changes occur within companies.

Successful family companies take a broader view. They *must* take a broader view. They recognize the relationship between people, processes and results, with people at the core. While numbers matter, there is a deeper story to those numbers, and they have to consider the broader implications to the organization and the individuals within it.

Family businesses also tend to have greater weight placed on the shoulders of the leaders or leadership teams. Leadership sets the tone for how everyone else in the organization sees themselves. Leaders must take the time to define roles, help people understand how they contribute to profitability, and create accountability with employees. While this is true of all types of companies, family dynamics make it even more important to establish clarity and accountability.

Additionally, successful family businesses are often flat organizations. They don't support bureaucracy like many publicly held companies do, and how individuals interact and relate to each other is critically important in creating a culture of communication. They've minimized their hierarchical structure and have instead fostered a linear environment where interaction can occur quickly at every level to affect internal and external outcomes.

Leadership sets the tone for how everyone else in the organization sees themselves.

But perhaps the greatest differentiator between family and publicly held businesses is the family business's true, authentic focus on people. They are far more attuned to the value and capacity of individuals, and that allows these companies to continue to grow in the success they achieve. They're not perfect. But they do understand the importance of the men and women who help them prosper.

Many family companies exist for one purpose: to preserve something, knowing that legacy will go on into the future. The primary exit strategy of nearly all of my clients is not the sale of their businesses. Each of them has had, and will continue to have, the opportunity to sell. Most say no, not because it is not a viable option but because of their extreme focus and commitment to their values. Quite simply, each owner has a specific vision regarding the future of his or her company. To these leaders, transferring a successful and profitable business to future generations is a responsibility they take seriously and willingly.

FROM SURVIVING TO THRIVING

In the late 90s, my work as a nationally recognized speaking professional involved traveling all over the country doing sales seminars. Even with my hectic speaking travel schedule, I was also the VP of sales and marketing at a company where I also held an ownership commitment. I was busy and exhausted. While I enjoyed what I was doing, I wanted more. I knew I needed to take a leap to transition from my position as VP into something new.

My speaking was contracted through a man named Carlton Masi, under his company, Masi Motivational. Carlton was a short, charismatic Italian guy who became my best friend in the world. He had a gift for taking the simplest concepts and convincing people they were the most wonderful ideas ever heard. As I began working with him, he quickly became my mentor. Who I am and what I do today would never have existed without him.

Carlton had a profound impact on me for many reasons but mostly because he helped me believe I could step into an arena outside of my own security. He taught me what it meant to thrive.

Before Carlton, I was what most would consider successful. I was working in a good job with a high salary. I was recognized for my achievements. But Carlton saw something in me that I didn't see in myself—he identified potential I couldn't, or wouldn't, see. He drew it out of me through mentoring, friendship and even tough love. I needed to transition my thinking, transition my life, to a place of thriving.

The best part? He taught me to constantly assess where I am and what I'm doing. He showed me that thriving is a lifelong pursuit. The quest never ends.

Before I met Carlton, I was surviving. "Successful" but surviving. And much like the younger me, many family businesses are doing the same. They convince themselves they are succeeding—and perhaps they are, at least on the surface. But if you were to dig a little deeper, prod the relationships that are foundational to growing and running a family business, question the plans and tactics used, and explore the intentionality of thought about the future, a truer picture would begin to emerge. And that picture would show companies that are merely subsisting. The scary part is that they can only continue for so long.

Things go smoothly until they don't. A company does well until it doesn't.

Surviving is working from what you *think* you know. For me, that meant continuing to live the life I'd lived. While I had a nagging feeling that there was something more, I thought I had it good. As a family business owner or leader, surviving means primarily dealing with all of the subjective factors you can possibly line up in your business. It's making decisions based on what's in front of you, decided solely on what seems clear to you from your experience or intuition. It's functioning at a level that says, "I know what I'm doing, so this is my decision."

> **Prod the relationships that are foundational to growing and running a family business.**

Why do I say, what you "think" you know? The fact is there is a big difference between what you think you know and what you could know, if you took the time to explore, to question, to confront.

I see this most often in hiring. Here's how most hiring processes work: Cover letters and résumés are reviewed, candidates are selected, interviews are completed. Hiring managers ask questions like, "Why do you want to work here? What is your greatest weakness as a professional?" Leaders think they know how to understand people. But most of the time, they don't. Still, they make hiring decisions that can markedly impact the organization's success, both in internal relationships and external measures like profitability.

You really can understand more about people before you hire them. It's more than résumés and open-ended questions; there are process-oriented approaches that can allow you to genuinely *know* the people you hire, the people you trust with your organization's success. If you want to move beyond simply surviving, you must be willing to introduce defined processes, often in areas where such definition seems foreign or unnecessary. An objective approach is especially important in hiring because people are the most complex part of any business.

A hospitality company call center in Fresno, California, has seen a drop in turnover and an increase in quality hires since incorporating a customized behavioral assessment that screens applicants for traits like friendliness, curiosity and multitasking. In 2013, 57 percent of large US companies used some sort of pre-assessment, up from 26 percent in 2001.[3] Leaders in these organizations recognized that much of what they needed to know about candidates wouldn't be revealed in interviews.

As an advisor, helping family companies understand the intricacies of these processes is part of what I do. But more than that, I help owners and leaders advance and prosper. Through our work together, they learn how to let go of subjectivity and embrace objectivity. It isn't easy, but it's often what separates the 3 percent who last into the fourth generation from the ones who fade away after just the second.

Thriving means you're willing to learn to maximize the capacity of your business. It's about exploring the greater dynamics that already exist in your business and learning what you can about people, processes, systems, cultures—all of the things that contribute to success.

This is one of the areas I enjoy most about my relationship with clients. I work with large, outwardly successful organizations to give them disruptive insights that cause them to think about what they don't know or aren't yet considering. I do so from the foundational belief that the mastery that built their business is uniquely different than the mastery needed to evolve it.

Imagine that you are standing facing away from a wall. Around your waist is a thick belt, and attached to that belt is a ten-foot bungee cord. You walk away from the wall, and soon you feel a tug. You dig your feet into the ground, push your body forward, and try with all your might to move farther away from the wall. You try to run, pushing your legs as hard as you can into the earth, and attempt to propel your-self forward. You can't. You're stuck.

> **Surviving only lasts so long. Thriving is what brings both longevity and fully actualized potential to an organization.**

Now, imagine someone replaces the bungee with a thin, stretchy cord. This isn't just any cord; it's extendable, so it'll go where you go. You walk away from the wall, expecting to feel a tug to stop. But the cord keeps extending. You're still connected to the wall, but you're also free to move, to continue forward.

If you're merely subsisting in your organization, you can only get so far until the bungee cord of subjectivity stops you in your path or even wrenches you back. Yet if you have a mindset of thriving, your extendable cord allows you to explore what's really out there. You're still attached to the wall—the company core—but you can move about freely, test your limits and explore the possibilities.

When I met Carlton, I was attached to a thick bungee. My potential was limited by the amount of give the tether afforded me. Carlton taught me that it was time to switch cords. And once I did, I was able to see my life with objectivity and explore possibilities I never would have considered before.

Surviving only lasts so long. Thriving is what brings both lon-gevity and fully actualized potential to an organization. Will you continue to be held back, or will you allow your organization—yourself—the opportunity to run?

DO MORE THAN FUNCTION

Let's say you drop dead tomorrow. Or maybe you just throw your hands up and head to a tropical island to live out your life. Whatever the case, you're not working anymore. As an owner or a leader in a family company, that means a critical piece of leadership is gone—*poof*—just like that.

Now, project five, ten, fifteen or more years into the future. Would you recognize your company? Would it still be around? Be honest. Take a moment to think about your business as it exists right now. Without you, would your organization continue well into the future?

If you are able to visualize your company surviving without you, you have already started to establish a mindset of sustainability. You may already be thriving or at least on your way there.

But if there is even the nagging sense that you wouldn't recognize the company or it wouldn't still be around, it's time to honestly assess where you are and make a change. Step back and think purposefully about whether there are steps you can take to become better tomorrow than you are today. And really, can't we all improve, no matter where we are?

You have the potential to grow.

One organization I worked with grew from $275 million in revenue and eighty salespeople to $1 billion and forty-eight salespeople, and it all began with approaching their current situation from a place of objectivity and honesty. Those are not stand-alone numbers. I could give similar case studies for nearly every client I've worked with. It's not me who makes these things happen; it's the leaders who want better for themselves and the people they lead. They recognize the opportunity for exponential growth. I'm fortunate to help them get there.

These leaders are committed to defining processes and exploring options beyond the entrepreneurial level. Entrepreneurs tend to think with their hearts and make decisions based on intuition. That works for a while, but it isn't a sustainable approach.

Instead, you must first approach your organization relationally. That might seem counterintuitive in today's world of process-driven companies, but in a family business, relationships are the pulse of the organization. If those relationships are a mess, the organization will be a mess. If both family and non-family members are functioning with mutual respect and in harmony, guess what? The business is likely succeeding. If you don't connect relationally first, there is little chance of ever connecting at a deeper level to impact the business.

You must also have a well-defined understanding of people and processes and how to fit them together to form the future you want for your organization. You have to be purposeful and intentional in defining roles within an organization and making sure there is a clear understanding of how people communicate. More than that, you must create a common language within your company so that everyone can communicate.

The aim is to avoid what I call "the lack of." If you lack definition, if you lack clarity, you will lack performance. If you are content with surviving, this will not present a problem for you. But if you know that you're capable of more and you believe someone could help you get there, then it's time to explore a clear approach to radically reenvision your organization.

It all starts with first understanding the unique conditions in a family business. And it relates back to—you guessed it—relationships.

2

Functional Dysfunction

For about a century and a half, scientists believed that being married increased the chances of good health. Studies dating back to as early as 1858 showed that unmarried people were more prone to dying from disease, while married couples were more likely to live long, healthful lives.

Study upon study in the twentieth century backed up this earlier research. While there were certainly some skeptics, the general sentiment, backed by science, was that married couples were happier, healthier people—what became known as the "marriage advantage."

But more recent findings admit an obvious caveat. For those in troubled relationships, the benefits don't exist. In fact, research has shown that a person in a bad marriage would be better off having not married at all. One study even suggested that a stressful marriage can be as bad for heart health as smoking.[1] It's not just miserable—it's harmful to one's well-being.

If a couple struggles in their marital relationship over several years, at some point they have learned to become what I call functionally dysfunctional. And if a couple doesn't work through the barriers that are preventing the marriage from thriving, eventually that relationship will either turn into a disdainful cohabitation or end in divorce.

Family companies that are simply surviving are much like bad marital relationships. They are functionally dysfunctional: They exist, but they are not achieving their full potential. Family relationships are negatively impacted, people are unhappy, and if the leadership team isn't careful, the company will eventually fail.

> **Preservation begins with admitting functional dysfunction exists. That simple admission starts the evolution process.**

Over years, decades or generations, these companies have shifted from the energy and raw enthusiasm of the founder to a level of dysfunction that permeates every level of the organization.

Happily married people don't just wake up one day feeling bitter and resentful. Organizations don't go from prospering to barely holding on in days or weeks. It happens over time, and it often occurs so gradually that no one really notices until the company is nearly beyond repair. It is a slow slide.

Most family companies—most families—have issues; there is usually dysfunction on some level. That's OK. It's normal. I'm not suggesting that you can eliminate organizational dysfunction completely. But the goal is to minimize the dysfunction. If you want to thrive, you've got to get real. You've got to deal with the realities of the business as it is, not as you wish it to be.

By all means, value your intuitive sense. But don't become myopic or blinded to dysfunction.

When I work with family businesses, I often begin by explaining, "We're going to start by identifying all of the dysfunction that exists within this group. It's not going to be pretty; I'll tell you that right now. You're going to consider it like group therapy. There are going to be feelings, and there might even be tears. It's going to get ugly before it gets better." That's the reality of confronting dysfunction.

Family companies have an almost universal desire to preserve love, legacy and leadership. This desire has a direct connection to the three areas of functional dysfunction: family dynamics, which deal with loving one another; preservation pressures, which connect to leaving a lasting legacy; and leadership dysfunction, which includes a distorted view, blind spots and subjective bias that can impact leadership in even the best-intentioned organizations. Preservation begins with admitting functional dysfunction exists. That simple admission starts the evolution process.

We will explore all three areas of functional dysfunction in depth, as well as some of the sub-challenges you'll face within each. As you read, ask, does this describe my company? Does this describe me? If you answer yes to either question, don't see it as a bad thing. View it as the first step: acknowledging dysfunction.

FAMILY DYNAMICS

If there's one thing you've taken away so far from our time together, it's probably this: Family dynamics make business more complex. We talked through some of the positives of the family structure in the previous chapter. From length of service to a real, authentic focus on people, your organization has some distinct advantages over publicly held companies. Yet it also probably has its issues.

Identifying functional dysfunction begins with giving a name to the problem. It's likely that you've had a feeling something is off for some time, but if you're like most leaders, you've had a hard time pinpointing the issue. In order to recognize and begin to deal with the dysfunction, you first must understand the unique challenges of your family business, from communication difficulties to generational dynamics. Let's explore those challenges.

DIFFICULTY COMMUNICATING

Family companies face a major challenge when it comes to communication: emotion.

A colleague told me a story about a family-owned school she worked at overseas. Run as a for-profit business, this school employed cousins, aunts, uncles and nieces to run the administration, teach classes and manage most major aspects of the school. Eventually, a rift formed between the owner and his aunt, the principal. The owner's cousin was a fifth-grade teacher and daughter to the principal, and she sided with her mom. Lawyers became involved. Family members took sides, mostly with the owner.

After several long months of disagreements, the principal and fifth-grade teacher were both fired on the same day, about an hour after the school day ended and most (but not all) kids had gone home. Shortly after, my colleague heard loud noises from across the building. The fifth-grade teacher screamed at her cousin, threw items across the room, and then ran out of the school in tears.

Minutes later, she got into one of the school's cars, backed into the street, and purposely rammed it into a wall across from the school.

This is an extreme example, but it's just an amplification of the emotional intensity that can occur within families. While emotion certainly exists in publicly held organizations,

You have to decide that communicating truly carries the level of importance it deserves.

there is no comparison to the depth of feeling that can exist in the family company. Emotions can run high, emotions can be repressed, emotions can be used to an unfair advantage and emotions can be revealed—especially at the worst possible times.

Understandably, emotion often gets in the way of effective communication. The best way I've found to deal with emotion is to establish an environment in which owners, leaders and management take the time to *really understand* each person at an individual level. In the story my colleague relayed, an honest attempt to understand each other might have saved a lot of drama.

Do you want to communicate and develop people in your organization in different ways, based on each person's individual style? I hear yes all the time. "Yes, I want to understand people," leaders tell me. "Yes, I want to develop people."

Let me put it another way. Have you objectively evaluated the people on your leadership and management teams through unbiased assessments and tools and then adjusted your communication based on those insights? This is the hardest work, understanding people as individuals, and yet it's often where organizations put the least amount of effort.

In order to eliminate the difficulty of communicating, to begin to find balance in the emotions that are sure to accompany family dynamics, you have to decide that communicating truly carries the level of importance it deserves.

The problem is organizations often value talking and communicating at the same level. Talking is not communicating. Talking is just a one-dimensional dialogue. Communicating involves the exchange of listening and talking.

It's an even greater challenge for families because of the emotion of relation. You see cases like a brother and sister who drive each other crazy because one is decisive and the other a reflective decision maker. There might be conflict because they are not taking the time to understand why they behave the way they do. Difficulty in communication occurs when people don't work to value and adapt their approach to each other as individuals; they simply want to attack the person, rather than solve the problem.

If my behavior is different than your behavior, guess what we're going to have? Conflict. If the motivations behind my behaviors are different than your motivations, what will we have? Conflict. If we want to avoid or solve conflict, you have to adapt and I have to adapt. This is known as behavioral adaptation. Values can't be adapted—they are what they are—but in overcoming communication challenges, it's important to look at both behaviors (how) and values (why). From there, individuals can meet somewhere in the middle and begin to work through communication concerns—how I prefer to do things versus how you prefer to do things. That is going to require true coaching, true development and true interaction.

If you're like many of the leaders I work with, you're likely thinking, "That takes too much time." Well, hold on for a second. If you want to maximize performance, you must work to encourage frequent, quality communication that maximizes people.

DIFFERENT GENERATIONS, DIFFERENT IDEAS

Recently, I spoke with a young man in his midthirties about politics. We'd had an enjoyable conversation. Then, he commented, "When I see one of these old politicians, I think to myself, 'Your time has passed; let somebody younger in with fresh ideas.'"

I stopped, startled. What, because they're old? Only a young person can have fresh ideas? I sure hope not, because at fifty-plus years of age, that means I should just stop what I'm doing right now.

New ideas come from everyone. When you start to dismiss someone's ideas just because the person is "old" or "from the past," you miss out on the opportunity to objectively evaluate what a person is saying.

I hear similar comments from the older generation. "She's too young to understand," or "He isn't old enough to have developed as a leader." And I can see it on their faces when a young person voices an opinion—a look that says, "Punk, you don't know anything."

It's not about when a person was born. It's about ideas and the exchange of knowledge.

Recently, my wife and I took a cruise to celebrate her fiftieth birthday. We cruised on the *Norwegian Jewel*, a massive ship measuring 965 feet long, 125 feet wide and 195 feet high and weighing over 93,000 tons. I had the opportunity to meet the captain, Niklas Persson, and the second officer, Matthew Deegan. Captain Persson was in his early forties and from Sweden, while Matthew was in his late twenties and from New Zealand. Both were instrumental in navigating a ship that housed 2,376 passengers and more than 1,100 crew members.

Captain Persson is one of the youngest individuals to earn the position of captain; the typical route of ascent is twenty or more years of captaining a cargo ship before moving to a passenger ship.

Instead, he fast-tracked his way to the Norwegian Cruise Line and eventually to the position of captain. Persson is a bright and personable individual who grew up on and around the water. Just because his ideas and abilities didn't follow the "typical path," it certainly doesn't mean he isn't valid or skilled as a captain.

When my wife and I boarded the ship, we didn't ask how old the captain and his crew were. If we had only considered age, imagine what we might have thought. Age isn't always an indicator of skills and abilities.

> It's important to value generational differences.

It's important to note that age isn't always a measure of experience, either. I know people in their fifties who have limited experience and people in their thirties who have made gaining experience their life's work.

The thing is, the generation gap is real, especially in family businesses. It's common to have a father passing the company down to a daughter and possibly even have a grandfather who is still living and has some sort of involvement in the organization. There may be uncles and aunts in leadership. The company may include cousins who are separated by a generation and freshly degreed nieces and nephews beginning their careers.

With four generations working together in the workplace—soon to be five—there is a disparity in motivations, attitudes and actions.[2] Millennials, born roughly between 1980 and 1999, make up the largest cohort in history.[3] With these wide ranges of generations—and with newer generations making up the bulk of workers—it's important to value generational differences. It's even more important to avoid using identity with different generations as a scapegoat for why the family isn't communicating.

There's no consideration for generation when a captain is communicating with the crew to navigate a ship through the fiords of Alaska. There is, however, an expectation of skill and ability. The captain and his team must communicate for safe passage through unpredictable Alaskan waters. Thousands of lives depend on it.

Two people can engage regardless of age, just like Captain Persson and Second Officer Deegan. You've surely watched a twenty-year-old and seventy-year-old engage effectively. In that interaction, each person isn't focusing on how old the other person is; they're each focusing on engagement. They're focusing on who the other person is. They're seeking to understand each other at an individual level.

Remember, it's about ideas. If you're part of the younger generation, ask yourself, do I value ideas from my older colleagues, or do I dismiss them all? If you're part of the older generation, ask yourself, do I value ideas from my younger colleagues, or do I dismiss them all?

Understanding the art of engagement—deeply connecting with all generations to bring fresh ideas—is crucial to supporting performance. If you're not engaging each generation to bring the best ideas, you're posing an either/or—either this generation or that generation. Let's make it *and* so all generations can bring novel approaches and perspectives to the table.

INTEGRATING FAMILY AND NON-FAMILY LEADERSHIP

Not all family companies bring in non-family leadership. I sometimes recommend it and I sometimes don't. But I have seen great success in certain instances where the family was willing to open up leadership to someone outside the family.

I worked with a client whose organization was family owned and family led, as opposed to being family owned and others led. Family members held all of the senior leadership positions. After applying methodology, resources and tools to objectively assess each leader's role and contribution to the organization, it became clear that one leader did not fit the operational role needed for the company. While this person could add value on the board, he wasn't the individual to run the company daily. I recommended finding a non-family leader, someone who was acceptable to the family and aligned with the culture, and we put together a definition of the position to help guide the decision.

What was critical in this process was first helping the family come to an agreement that there needed to be a non-family leader brought in, and second, finding a person who was a great fit for both the family and culture of the organization. The family had to get a good "vibe" from that person. If they didn't, forget it. No matter how "HR correct" a person might be, the family must have buy-in, or they won't invest in the success of the individual.

For an individual joining an organization, family companies can be extremely tough to integrate into. These leaders have to overcome hurdles other people don't have to overcome. I've watched family members—or even long-serving non-family employees—meander past hurdles and be deemed acceptable while other individuals jump fifty more hurdles and are still considered unacceptable. Bringing someone in from the outside, whether a completely new hire or by promoting from within the organization, means the current leadership needs to be intentional about onboarding and integrating that person into both the company and defined role.

Existing leaders also need to understand how difficult integrating into a culture can be. The adversary of integration is longevity in the culture. These long-term leaders often forget how insulated the culture has become. In order to integrate someone new, they must be purposeful.

As a leader, you must also be deliberate about integration. Treat it like a process and define the major cores of the culture. Create a schedule by which those cores are reviewed and discussed with the new leader. The cores must both be understood and demonstrated as being "core to the fabric" or "core to the soul" of who that person is. It's not enough to talk about it. At the level of integration, it must be demonstrated. It must be authentic. The standard bearers of culture will know intuitively if it's being faked.

Companies would be well served to designate someone to be the "cultural Sherpa," the cultural integrator, for the new person. Sherpas exist to give climbers the best chance of reaching the summit. They don't guarantee the climber's triumph; they simply decrease the risk of death and increase the potential of success. This is the same of a cultural Sherpa. Any cultural integration that is left to happen accidentally or by the new person's own accord has a greater chance of failure. The cultural Sherpa guides the new hire to successfully integrate into the company.

UNDERSTANDING PEOPLE OBJECTIVELY

I have a picture in my office of my daughter. In the photo, she is around sixteen, a young and happy teen. I love that picture.

One day, I was on the phone with her. She's now a professional in her midtwenties with a bachelor's and a master's degree. We had been talking about incorporating her into Perpetual Development, the business I run with my wife, Trudy.

After a while, there was a pause on her end. Then, she said, "Dad, you don't find me credible at all in having potential to work with your company, do you?"

"No, that's a bit extreme. I don't see it that way," I replied quickly. "But you have to understand that every day, I'm staring at a picture of you when you were sixteen years old. Sometimes it's hard for me to look beyond that picture and see what you've become."

There was another pause before she said, "Then I suggest you change the picture."

She was right. She's still right. I haven't changed the picture, but I have worked hard to change the way I see her. She's not my baby anymore. She's an adult with an education she has worked hard to achieve. She has practical professional experience. She has become a driven, intelligent and extremely talented young woman who is now working in her area of passion and expertise.

Not long after that conversation and after going through the same methodology and assessments I recommend to my clients, I hired her as marketing curator—and it's one of the best decisions I've made.

As a leader in a family company, no matter how objective you believe you are about family members, unless you are willing to introduce an objective assessment, you are still highly subjective. Granted, some people have intuitive senses that are more highly developed than others—their awareness is greater. But unless you are a species other than human, you are working from your experiences and opinions. We all are.

Father, mother, son, daughter, brother, sister, wife, husband—whatever the relationship, the hardest thing to do is overcome subjectivity, because here's what happens: You will talk to them and think about them differently unless you deliberately decide to change your approach. You will likely say things to family members you would never say to others because you're constantly waging battle with your view of them.

Objectivity does not come naturally. It must be worked at. And as I've seen over and over again, it can only be achieved through outside help: advisors, assessments and other means of approaching emotional relationships with an unbiased perspective. It's about changing the picture that's freeze-framed in your head or sitting on your office shelf.

CONFRONTING PERFORMANCE ISSUES AND STILL LOVING EACH OTHER

"With love for mankind and hatred of sins." That's what St. Augustine wrote in the fifth century. Over time, it became more popularly recited, "Love the sinner, but hate the sin."[4]

In a family business, it's important to remember this principle. You can love a family member who is underperforming in his role while still hating the performance issues themselves.

When there are performance issues in a family company, things get tricky. Confronting problems is never fun, but it's even less fun when it's your cousin or sister, son or stepdaughter. Yet performance is an expectation of business. Everyone must perform. Love for your family member aside, if she is not delivering, you need to deal with her underperformance just like you would with a non-family member.

I often say to the leaders I work with, "I don't hire you. I don't fire you. I don't give you a raise. I don't determine whether you've been successful or unsuccessful in the performance of your job. As it relates to objectivity, the objective understanding of who you are, you have met the person (me) who is going to help you define that in the organization."

You can address performance issues similarly with objectivity. It starts with establishing an environment in which there is a clear light to respectfully and appropriately address performance at every level, regardless of relationship. That's what you would do with someone who is not related. Why take a different approach with relatives?

What's interesting is that while some leaders dread these conversations about performance issues, the results will tend to exceed their expectations. Two things usually happen when approaching performance objectively. First, the person with the performance issue feels that someone finally gets him. Second, the person feels like a huge weight is off his shoulders.

Underperforming leaders have often been waiting for a conversation about their positions, to express that they feel like they're inappropriately placed or have other challenges that are preventing them from doing their jobs. Rarely are family members flat out bad for the company. More often, they are simply a bad fit for their positions.

Whatever you do, don't avoid dealing with problems, especially with family members. The sooner you deal with them, the better off everyone will be.

It's true family dynamics can get in the way of growth and success. But you don't have to accept things as they are. By identifying where functional dysfunction exists and dealing with challenges objectively and effectively, you'll strengthen the family and the organization. You'll begin building a pathway towards sustainability that will last for generations to come. And best of all, you'll still love each other.

PRESERVATION PRESSURES

Perhaps the greatest pressure family business owners and leaders face is preservation. The statistics, as we have learned, offer a grim view of the likelihood of a company surviving past the third generation. Yet for those companies who do last, there is great pressure to preserve the legacy of the family business while still being open to the opportunities of the future. From the family name to culture to continuing what's been built, preservation becomes not only important but necessary to the survival and success of the business.

Functional dysfunction occurs when family members don't appreciate or honor being part of the family business. One of the biggest pressures? The family name.

YOU ARE YOUR NAME

A couple of years ago, I was flying back from a client engagement. The airline had upgraded me to first class. The flight attendant made her rounds, greeting each customer by name. Finally, she arrived at my seat.

"Mr. Patmos, is that correct?" she asked. I replied yes, and she continued by welcoming me to the flight. As she walked away, I felt a tap on my shoulder and turned around.

"Did I hear your name correctly, that it's Patmos?" the woman behind me asked.

"Yes, that's me," I replied.

"Was your grandfather a doctor?"

"Yes, he was."

"Is he from Adrian, Michigan?" she continued.

"He was, yes, before he passed away. He's buried there," I replied. My grandfather had been well known in the area, his name recognized throughout the entire community.

"He delivered me!" she exclaimed. She went on to explain that her parents had spoken fondly of my grandfather; she even remembered that a hospital library was named after him. As I listened to her talk, it was clear that my grandfather had a great impact on her family. And just by association, by being his grandson, I was somehow a part of him, a part of his legacy.

That's the power of a family name.

Like me, you don't get to choose your name or the associations that come with it. In a thriving family company, there is often a strong positive association with a last name, even if that last name isn't part of the company name itself. Your name isn't negotiable—unless, of course, you want to change it and remove yourself from the business altogether.

I often hear from emerging leaders, "I am who I am. I want my life to remain private." What I've found so intriguing is how quickly people are willing to dismiss the accountability for who they are, the name they possess, all in the quest for individuality.

If you carry the name, or if you embody the name through leadership as a non-family member, you represent the brand. If you don't want that accountability, don't claim it at any level. But if you want some of the perks that go along with the success

> You don't get to choose your name or the associations that come with it.

that name has brought, understand that you have an obligation and accountability to preserve the name and what it represents.

As an owner or leader in a family company, people are always assessing how you act. Whether you're out to dinner with your family or in a boardroom, others will recognize you. They'll recognize the name. And they'll attach value judgments that may impact the sentiment towards your organization. In a sense, the name becomes its own entity.

Really, it all comes down to being a well-respected person inside and outside company walls: making good decisions, caring for people, and being purposeful and intentional in your choices. Understanding the value and pressure that go along with preservation of the family name. And, of course, remembering that your name, whether you like it or not, carries with you—even when you're hundreds of miles away on an airplane home.

IT'S ALL ABOUT CULTURE

In the 90s, Jack Welch, then CEO of General Electric, had a radical—some may call it brutal—strategy. Each year, he ranked the employees in his organization and fired the bottom 10 percent. He essentially created self-generated turnover to thin the pool of people who were underperformers.

There is no way under any circumstance, in any form or fashion, that I would ever advise a family company to operate that way. Ever.

What Welch did with his strategy was create a culture. Not a people-focused culture; not a culture of growth and innovation. He created a culture of fear. Everyone at General Electric knew that people were going to lose their jobs each year. Who wants to work—to live—like that?

Sure, proponents of Welch's approach can point to the numbers: Company revenue grew fivefold to $130 billion.[5] I understand that's hard to argue with. I get his intent and purpose, but that intent and purpose are in opposition to many family companies.

Successful family businesses create a culture that is performance oriented to thrive and maximize, not stagnate and survive. And they do that with one common element: their people. Welch would probably tell you he was an advocate for people. I call bull. He was an advocate for profits and process.

> **What defines an effective business culture is a commitment to people and a longer-term view than a quarterly dividend.**

What defines an effective business culture, be it family or otherwise, is a commitment to people and a longer-term view than a quarterly dividend. It is discipline and patience applied to the success of an organization through people, by people, with people, for people. Not in a soft way, or in exclusion of process and fiscal management, but quite the opposite. It's done in a completely objective way that looks at every dimension of the business in a realistic manner. Doing so allows you to define a culture in which people are confident and secure.

The pressure to preserve culture is perhaps one of the greatest pressures of all: continuing a people- and process-centered culture that will last for generations.

The leaders I work with treat the people in their companies like they are an extension of their family. Do you? It's true that not all people are gifted in interacting with others, but if that's not your natural bent, you can't just avoid the need to focus on people. You can't ignore people, or the culture of your organization will erode.

Ask yourself as you're evaluating the company culture, the foundation of your organization: What is the cultural foundation? How has culture been developed? What does that culture look like? How will it evolve? As I help leaders think through the process of understanding and defining their culture, I focus on people, competitive advantage, differentiated approach, resourcefulness, processes—every element of how the culture serves the organization to help build clarity.

PRESERVING THE PAST WHILE STAYING OPEN TO THE FUTURE

If I could go back to thirty-two-year-old me and change one thing about how I functioned as a professional, it would be this: I would have been more direct about what was right, what was wrong and what needed to be changed. While I didn't think I knew it all, I certainly had a lot of room to grow in self-awareness. As a leader responsible for a significant segment of business in a large company in the Midwest, I

> **People are often afraid to deviate from what's expected.**

toed the line. I knew that if I voiced disagreement, it would meet resistance and resentment, so I kept quiet. And this was at a good company I still have the utmost respect for. Even there, the culture didn't allow for openness of communication at all levels.

Family companies can be similar. People are often afraid to deviate from what's expected. It's likely that your organization has a rich history and way of doing things—set expectations for how aspects of the company function and how people are supposed to behave in accordance with that structure. But if the people in your business are simply toeing the line, following the rules so to speak, they're not fully contributing to the accountability of their positions.

Instead of supporting bureaucracy, family businesses with great cultures supported by great people exist to support performance. True performance. Instead of having an attitude of protectionism, of safeguarding "the way we do things," they enable people to bring unique ideas and fresh perspectives to the table. Of course, I'm not suggesting that every person should feel comfortable throwing around ideas without regard. It's not a free-for-all. I'm simply saying that when you operate a linear platform, the primary perspective really is performance, not bureaucracy.

There are two ways family companies can support true performance. First, utilize collaboration teams. These teams are given a project emphasis that is to initiate or improve something within the company. The projects aren't pie in the sky. They are tangible, and the teams are expected to come up with actionable approaches that will enhance performance, advance new opportunities, reduce expense, improve profitability or grow sales. Senior leadership determines the project emphasis for collaboration teams so that time isn't wasted developing "nice ideas" that don't really contribute to the expected outcomes.

Second, pose a monthly idea or innovation challenge—essentially, create an idea incubator. Establish parameters and details so there isn't a free-for-all. In this situation, a diverse group of no more than seven individuals from throughout the company are brought together with owners and/or executive leadership to review a problem or initiative and arrive at a strategy and approach for improvement. Again, these are tangible issues with actionable approaches.

In both scenarios, the teams develop a recommended game plan complete with a time line and bring it back for discussion, collaboration, confirmation and implementation. The final strategy incorporates details on agreed measures of performance, payback, profitability and expense reduction. You can adapt these two ideas to your company's needs to spur communication and collaboration within your organization.

As you work to support performance, also consider if you are a "what" or "why" leader. Most often, leaders will define the what of their companies, which creates less emotional connection than the why. Instead, focus on helping people understand their why. Millennials, in particular, are looking for organizations in which they can understand the why. Why am I working this way? Why am I doing this job? Why am I in this position? Why does this business exist, and why do we do what we do? When you communicate with people in this way, in addressing the why, you grab the hearts and minds of people. I call it head share, heart share and hand share.

A great example of this takes place within miles of my home. Each year in Tempe, Arizona, there is a memorial event marking 9/11. Volunteers set up three thousand US flags in memory of those who lost their lives in the September 11 attacks. Imagine if there were only head share (thinking just about the task) involved in setting up the flags. People would understand the task, but they wouldn't have fully committed in their hearts and through the use of their hands. The minute the work is connected to the three thousand lives lost in the attacks and the memory of 9/11, there is a complete understanding of why and an engagement that leads to head share (thinking), heart share (connecting internally) and hand share (volunteering and setting up the flags). Each year, people from around the valley volunteer to participate. Why? Because of what each flag represents.

When you grab the head share, heart share and hand share of people, you're taking them into account in totality. You're saying, "Here's why what you do matters to us. You are not just one of four hundred people in this company; here is how you're making a difference."

In short, look for ways of moving forward—of seeking out new ideas that connect to a person's why while still preserving the culture and legacy of your organization. In order to advance, you must support a structure that allows for voices and opinions to be heard.

PASSING THE BUSINESS TO THE NEXT GENERATION

I once witnessed the emotional breakdown of a young leader who was the president of a company. There was so much pressure on her to take over the family business, to follow in her father's footsteps, that it landed her in therapy.

Each generation of owners feels immense pressure to pass the family business on. Children of those owners feel the pressure too. Many parents see the family business as a gift they give their children, something they can pass down. If a son or daughter resists the gift, or even fails at the attempt to take over leadership, parents don't understand why. There is a whole lot of judgment going on, all in the name of preservation.

The first thing to acknowledge is that just because someone is a family member, it doesn't make them qualified to lead. They may not even want to lead. But if you are lucky enough to have a willing and able family member, or to be that family member yourself, passing the business on is about more than just signing legal documents.

An owner I worked with started grooming his son for leadership at the ripe age of twenty-two, preparing the young man to someday take over the business. The father knew the son wasn't ready then, but he would be someday. Why not spend ten or more years developing that young man into a leader who will honor the culture and past of the organization while looking forward to the exciting future ahead?

Too often, owners fall in love with the idea of their relatives taking over. I encourage you to not just love the idea but also love the execution of that idea. Love the work that goes into making it happen.

Think about generational transition with the same deliberate approach that you would take with a new product, line or service. The key here is consistency. It concerns me how casually some owners approach the transition of their businesses, often by ignoring or denying the inevitable. Some seem to believe the situation will magically take care of itself over time. It won't. Most of the leaders I work with would never operate their companies with that kind of casualness. I encourage them to give the same energy to transitioning that they put into products, service or customers.

> I encourage you to not just love the idea but also love the execution of that idea.

Given the risk involved with a leadership transition, it seems natural that planning and strategy would be requirements to ensure transitional success. But I have seen too many situations where this is not the case. If you're an owner dealing with transitional leadership, here are seven important recommendations:

1. Decide on the type of transition. Will this be a family member or non-family member? Internal advancement or external selection?

2. Determine the time line required for effective transition, given all business factors, conditions and requirements.

3. Develop a formal transitional process for the incoming leader, including year-to-year and/or month-to-month requirements and action steps for the determined duration of transition.

4. Establish benchmarks of success that include specific details of accomplishment, given the culture of the company. This could include working within and understanding multiple areas of the company, building key relationships, or leadership mentoring with associates and leaders, to name a few.

5. Communicate relentlessly in formal and informal settings about anything and everything that needs to be understood, clarified or dealt with to prevent blind spots for the leadership transition.

6. Select an external advisor who has extensive internal knowledge of the company to provide support and guidance with an objective perspective.

7. Assess the integration progress at established intervals to confirm mutual agreement on moving forward. The objective is to identify any significant disconnects sooner than later and address those appropriately.

Throughout the process, continue talking. Continue planning and executing the plan. But above all, continue being intentional in the transition.

LEADERSHIP DYSFUNCTION

I worked with a family business owner I greatly respect for a number of reasons but especially because of this: He didn't leave his future leaders to flounder upon his departure. He didn't say, "I'm retiring next week, kids. Good luck." Instead, he gave them four to five years to transition from him as a single, charismatic leader to a distributed leadership platform. He engaged outside help to assist in forming an executable plan that gave his team the best chance for success. He recognized that it had taken him decades to build the business—why then step away without the proper care and planning the transition deserved?

Unfortunately, this isn't the norm. As owners age and retire, they all too often leave a person or team in charge with very little training and preparation. There needs to be a much more formal definition of transitioning and aligning people to positions. In my client's case, the largest part of that transition involved training the leaders who would take his place.

While the average tenure of a CEO in a publicly traded company is six years, top leaders in family businesses often stay for twenty to twenty-five years.[6] This is both a strength and a weakness. These long-term leaders are typically immersed in the culture and dedicated to the company, but it can be difficult for them to adopt new technologies and techniques. And with no plans to retire anytime soon, the greatest detriment may be that leaders aren't training upcoming leaders purposefully and intentionally.

As daughters, sons, nieces and nephews enter the business, they are molded by the previous generations, sometimes without much care or attention towards leadership development at all. The new leaders are instead expected to learn on the job. Or family members are accepted into the organization without formal education, experience or outside success—it's assumed they'll flourish in the family enterprise, even if they haven't proven themselves elsewhere.

Will people prosper simply because they have the same name or relationship to the family business? Can people truly thrive when their experiences, learning and growth come primarily from inside the walls of their company? And moreover, how can they sincerely grow and succeed in a global marketplace when they only have experiences and insights from within their company, city or state?

The assumption that someone will be a success "just because (insert reason here)" leads not only to a lack of true awareness but also to experiential blindness. It's an attitude that says, "I know what I know in the place I'm familiar with, but I know nothing beyond the boundaries and barriers I've created for myself."

You can't lead in the diverse environment of today's marketplace if you limit your experiences. Consider a cruise ship, much like the one my wife and I traveled on to Alaska. Ships of that size have staff from more than sixty different countries. The ship is like a mini United Nations, carrying thousands of passengers from all over the world, each with varying cultural backgrounds. More than once, I've witnessed the frustration of passengers who only knew the "view from their windshield." Their limited perspectives caused them to become angry, irritated or otherwise put out, often only because they were unable to see the situation from another person's cultural perspective. Things that are normal to one person aren't to another. Dysfunctional interactions occur not because the people themselves are bad but usually because they haven't taken the time to look beyond their windshields.

For leaders to flourish within a family company, they must expand their view, and they must train future leaders with a wide perspective, as well. There is power in longevity and knowledge within a company or industry. But there is frailty in lacking experiences beyond the boundaries of what a person or company knows. Avoiding leadership dysfunction means you must truly *seek learning*, not just intellectually but experientially.

Leaders must expand their view and train future leaders with a wide perspective.

Each of my clients began with a local reach. Today, without exception and regardless of industry or type of company, each does business throughout North America or globally. They have flourished not because they have limited their growth but because they have expanded their reach, influence and boundaries.

Interestingly, when I point out this idea of professional growth beyond boundaries to owners and executives, they pause for a moment as they consider the concept. Then, one of three things occurs:

1. They continue to ignore the connection of growth beyond boundaries related to people and yet still can't understand why their business isn't growing at all.

2. They have an aha moment about why they aren't growing their business beyond those boundaries.

3. They already recognize the connection of growth beyond boundaries related to their business and want to see that continue by expanding the development of their people beyond boundaries.

Dysfunctional leadership limits itself to what's known. Maximized leadership seeks to develop beyond the boundaries of their company or industry, no matter where the company is located.

To begin maximizing your own leadership, start with objectivity. Evaluate your business objectively. Be honest about when you plan to step away from the company and transition leadership. Plan for the unexpected, like a sudden death or debilitating injury. Develop a transition plan years before it seems necessary, and stick with it.

> **Functional dysfunction has its grip on most family-owned businesses in some form or another.**

When it comes to training up future leaders, be objective in assessment and diligent in training. Even if you've already placed someone in a position, ask yourself, where do I see this person fitting best, and do I have a process to define that role? Aligning people with positions through assessments and resources is one of the greatest ways to bring clarity to an organization.

Treat family as you would nonfamily, being honest in your appraisal of their successes and failures within the organization. Work to understand people, and methodically develop and train people who can maximize their performance. Leadership dysfunction doesn't have to be the standard—it should be the exception. Great leadership continually pushes beyond boundaries.

Functional dysfunction has its grip on most family-owned businesses in some form or another. I have yet to come across a family business that is running perfectly without issues at some level—and that's because such a company does not exist and never will. Yours is not exempt. But while functional dysfunction is a challenge to be taken seriously, it's not a death sentence. There is a bright side.

THE BRIGHT SIDE

In 2015, Dan Price, CEO of Gravity Payments, a privately held company in Seattle, made a decision. It was a decision he'd been considering for months, one he'd sought mentor and expert advice on, one that kept him up for nights on end, considering the consequences.

The day of his announcement, a Monday just like any other Monday, he gathered his 120-person staff together. As he walked to the front of the group, the staff grew quiet.

"Effective immediately, we're going to put a scaled policy into place," he told his employees, "and we're going to have a minimum $70,000 pay rate for everyone that works here." He added that he'd be taking his salary down to the minimum $70,000 until company profits went back up, a steep cut from the nearly $1 million he was bringing in annually.

There wasn't much of a reaction as the group tried to absorb what he was saying. Dan went on to explain the details of the rate increase, and the shock and excitement began to dawn on each person's face, one at a time. When Dan finished talking, the room erupted in cheers as the staff leapt to their feet for a standing ovation.[7]

Dan did something that could only happen in a privately held or family-owned business. He made a decision based not on money but on values. He was troubled knowing that certain members of his staff, while compensated fairly per market standards, were struggling to pay their bills. So, he decided to do something about it.

I'm not endorsing his idea or suggesting that every business make a similar decision. But Dan's story is a wonderful example of what you *can* do as a family business owner. You can live your values—really and truly live your values—not just through words and promises but through actions too.

I chose to build my career around working with family businesses for a simple reason. There is so much potential in these companies not only to grow and thrive but to do so in a way that honors heritage, respects history, looks towards the future and values people. They get to make decisions that preserve love, legacy and leadership. Like the organizations I work with, yours is unique *because it's a family business.* You can make choices like Dan's, if you so choose. Or not. But the point is that you have the ability to align with your values.

You can live your values in what you give back to people. Or in the way you deal with the most contentious of situations in your organization or community. Or in resolving conflicts in your organization. Or in how you compensate people or give them unique opportunities. The options are endless because you have the freedom to live a values-driven life and lead with values-driven leadership.

Family-owned businesses have other advantages, as well. They can make decisions with more immediate outcomes in mind, rather than having to go through bureaucratic hoops to make things happen. They can—and must—think with a long-term view of the health of the company, rather than the short-term shareholder dividend.

Moreover, they have greater retention, which means less chaos trying to fill those slots and onboard new people. But it's more than just low turnover—they have a more engaged workforce. When people feel like they are participating, it is an example of a family company run well. Opportunity, growth, a future. Employees know that while they're in position A right now, they could be in position B and later C because there is room to grow. These organizations have the ability to build on the longevity and consistency of people within the company because people are around longer and more engaged in the success of the organization and the individuals in it.

Family businesses are a part of a legacy. And they're also part of building a new legacy for future generations. They make a difference in the lives of people and inspire commitment to drive performance. That's what you offer as an owner or leader in a family company—the opportunity to make a difference. The opportunity to value people and grow an organization that is not only profitable and successful monetarily but does so with respect and regard to its greatest asset: its people.

RADICALLY IMPROVE YOUR BUSINESS WITH A PERFORMANCE-DRIVEN MINDSET

Clearly, as a family company owner or leader, you have a lot of challenges to work through and advantages to draw from. I advise family organizations all the time that are struggling to find balance, grow their strengths and minimize their weaknesses. One way to begin to do so is to adopt a performance-driven mindset.

Even big business is getting this idea. General Electric realized in 2014 that its focus was too diversified. Brutal firing tactics of the 80s and 90s aside, it had become a company so far from its core that it was almost unrecognizable. The company had formed GE Capital in the 1930s as a platform to sell General Electric products, but it soon drifted further and further from its purpose, doing everything from financing fast-food chains to owning office buildings—a far cry from selling refrigerators and washing machines.

Finally, the company leadership said enough is enough. They wanted coherence. As an article in *Fortune* put it, "The world's biggest diversified conglomerates are finally realizing that combining entirely dissimilar businesses in one company almost never works."[8] In order to support true performance, General Electric needed to focus on what it did best.

In many ways, General Electric was like an untrained Clydesdale horse. Clydesdales are magnificent creatures known for their power and beauty, a standard of presentation unique to that specific type of horse. They are usually well-cared-for, trained to near perfection and almost regal in their mannerisms.

Picture for a moment that you are standing in a field, and you see a group of fifty Clydesdales, running in different directions, bucking wildly with a fierce and frightened look in their eyes. Their manes are scruffy and unkempt, and even from a distance, you can see dirt caked on their legs and sides. Your first instinct would probably be to run and hide. Your second reaction might be, "Wait, this seems really off. This isn't how Clydesdales are supposed to act—something is wrong."

Clydesdales have a standard of performance. They are raised with a performance-driven mindset, a level of excellence that is unmatched and rarely wavers.

Like a pack of wild Clydesdales, General Electric needed to remove the disorder and refocus to see greater success.

Similarly, people in an organization can work in synchronicity of purpose or they can run amuck. If you have a group of fifty people scurrying in fifty different directions, doing their own jobs and not understanding the totality of the organization, they're like a bunch of horses running around madly. People may be working hard, but they're not pulling the same cart, seeing the standard of excellence. Getting individuals to work together, to understand the excellence that drives performance and their roles in the organization—that's the performance-driven mindset.

At its core, a performance-driven mindset is about valuing and maximizing the capacity of people in the positions they are best aligned to and clearly connecting how what they do contributes to their success and the success of the company. Of course, this mindset is most effective when the company itself has clarity around its purpose. McKinsey research has shown that investing in this mindset pays off—literally. An analysis of hundreds of global businesses showed that initiatives to boost talent, strengthen values and reinforce corporate culture directly improve the bottom line.[9]

> A performance-driven mindset is about valuing and maximizing the capacity of people.

To be clear, this mindset does not tolerate bad behavior or poor performance. I am not anti-termination. Clarity of accountability and ongoing communication about what that accountability requires has a way of either bringing people to the awareness required to advance their performance or thinning the herd of underperformers. A company that fosters the performance-driven mindset sets a pathway for those individuals to be weeded out. They'll go to organizations where they don't have to try so hard or care so much.

A performance-driven mindset can radically improve a family business for a simple reason: When you're committed to identifying and understanding the factors that can contribute to success— discipline and drive being primary—you help maximize people in a mutually beneficial relationship with the organization. It's a win-win.

Moreover, the mindset can improve communication and processes while expanding capabilities within your organization. It can help you grow the company more expediently, with greater definition, stronger commitment from people and an adaptable strategy. You'll get where you want to go sooner. And you'll be able to do so all while dealing with the cyclical nature of business with greater continuity and consistency.

Relentless pursuit. That's the phrase I'd like you to put up on your wall or repeat as your mantra each morning. Radically improving your family business is about the relentless pursuit of excellence. You must be willing to work through painful moments and face areas of functional dysfunction to reach the highest potential for your organization, your people and yourself.

When I think of this opportunity for growth, I'm reminded of a quote by Olympic athlete Wilma Rudolph: "Never underestimate the power of dreams and the influence of the human spirit. We are all the same in this notion: The potential for greatness lives within each of us."

Rudolph was a triumph in her own right. The twentieth of twenty-two children, she spent her childhood paralyzed by polio and battled scarlet fever and double pneumonia. While doctors believed she would never walk again, she wasn't about to give up. At age twelve, she could walk again and began playing sports. Just four years later, she competed in her first Olympic games as part of the American 4 x 100 relay, taking home a bronze metal. Eight short years later, she became an Olympic champion.[10]

We've spent the better part of this chapter analyzing the challenges you face in owning or running a family business. They are real. But there are also great advantages, as we've explored too. It all comes back to the spirit of the person—you, as a leader, and those you lead alongside—and the company. Sure, there are companies that are bigger and badder by definition, but they lack the spirit that is at the heart of companies like yours.

> **Radically improving your family business is about the relentless pursuit of excellence.**

Resilience, drive, dedication, commitment—the same qualities that propelled Rudolph forward to achieve what seemed impossible are the foundation of family companies. Are you ready to take the step forward? When principles, values and actions are aligned, that's when radical performance is possible.

3

Adopt the Thriving Mindset

In 2015, *Fortune* magazine published a list of the world's fifty greatest leaders. You would probably recognize many of the names on the list: Tim Cook, CEO of Apple; LeBron James, forward for the Cleveland Cavaliers; Bill and Melinda Gates, founders of the Bill & Melinda Gates Foundation; and Mark Zuckerberg, founder and CEO of Facebook.[1]

"Governments are failing, companies are under siege, and age-old institutions are losing their grip," the editorial reads. "How do you lead in a time when everyone is a free agent, following his own star? We've found 50 living lessons."

While the list includes many deserving individuals, I still couldn't help scratching my head while reading some of the names. Pop star Taylor Swift? *Tonight Show* host Jimmy Fallon? There's no doubt these individuals have impacted society. But to include them as part of the fifty greatest leaders in the entire world seems a bit of a stretch to me.

Noticeably absent from the list are the men and women I work with every day—individuals who are just as influential, just as passionate and just as dedicated. Yet they aren't flashy. They haven't gone viral. What they do isn't sexy. And believe me, they would balk at the idea of being called one of the fifty greatest leaders in the world, even though I could list several who deserve the honor.

To them, success isn't a *me* thing; it's an *us* thing. It's a result of the people in their businesses who have gotten them to where they are today.

The primary difference I see in the companies I work with is that they have adopted a mindset that sets them apart from other organizations in their fields. The key differentiator is their focus on people. These leaders are constantly asking themselves, how can we maximize people for a performance-driven culture and create a distinct competitive advantage?

It wouldn't be fair to leave out the publicly traded family companies who began with and continue to operate with a clear focus on people. But the goals and objectives of those organizations are often influenced at some point by the lure of the stock exchange. Visit the website of The J.M. Smucker Company, a publicly held company that is best known for Smucker's® jelly and has been family run for four generations. On the same page that lets customers "Learn More About Our Company," you'll see links to history, culture . . . and an investments page that lists the current stock prices.[2] The organization is clearly still concerned about having a "culture of appreciation. A *family* sense of sharing in a job well done . . . [w]here every person makes a difference."[3] But even with good intentions, the company has to answer to the shareholders in a way privately held companies don't.

Visit the site of SC Johnson, and you'll see a different picture. As the company puts it, "SC Johnson has been led by the Johnson family for five generations. . . . Being a family company also means we put core values—such as integrity, respect, fairness and trust—above everything else. Being privately held enables us to focus on doing what's right for the next generation, not just the next quarter's earnings report."[4]

Being publicly traded certainly isn't a bad thing. It's different. Privately held companies require a distinct mindset to grow and thrive in a way that fits their core values.

This mentality is part of why I am so passionate about working with the leaders I advise. They demonstrate a keen business sense coupled with a dedication to people that is unparalleled elsewhere in the business world. Sure, family businesses have their challenges to overcome, but these organizations are solid at the core. And the core is people.

Through my work with these thriving family companies, I've identified nine elements to what I call a "thriving mindset." As you read each of the nine attributes, ask yourself, is this how I lead my organization? If so, how can I develop ways to continue doing so? If not, what do I need to change about my leadership?

If you're like most family company owners and leaders, you are likely at a place where you know a mindset evolution is necessary. Often, this is because a circumstance or event has caused you to realize that how you've been handling things isn't working anymore (or maybe it never really worked to begin with). You might perceive that there's a better way to achieve the growth you envision.

Evolving your mindset requires a mental commitment. It requires execution. And in the end, your mindset shift will set the stage for helping people and your company flourish.

ATTRIBUTE 1: SEE SALES AND PROFITS AS OUTCOMES, NOT TARGETS

All businesses, family owned or not, have to face a reality: We live in a results-driven world. There are four aspects of this reality:

1. *Results are driven by your actions.* What you do produces a result, either good or bad.

2. *Actions are driven by your thoughts.* Decisions aren't involuntary; thoughts are involved in every decision to act.

3. *Thoughts are driven by your thinking.* The level of intention and time spent thinking results in motivation, which drives actions, which produce results.

4. *Thinking is driven by the intent to make something happen.* Often, problems spur us to spend time thinking . . . or even avoid spending time thinking. The leaders who thrive know that in order to achieve the results they're after, they must spend time on the front end—contemplating.

The intent, if we are considering the reality of business, is simple: to achieve sales and profits. But a difference in family companies that thrive is that they see sales and profits as *outcomes* of everything else they do. What do I mean by that?

The standard course is that sales and profit growth are thought of as targets to be achieved. That means that decisions and choices are driven by hunt-kill-eat mentality. If the hunting goes well, everything's fine. If it doesn't go well, people metaphorically go hungry and then a lot of decisions are made without regard to broader implications; the leader only considers whether sales and profit goals are being met.

In order to thrive, you must see people as the number one focus. Sales and profits are an outgrowth of

Sales and profits become outcomes, not targets.

successfully investing in people and creating a performance-driven culture. Increased revenue is a result of treating people well, and of an environment where people want to do what they do and who they are is aligned with the accountabilities of their positions for superior performance.

While the reality of business doesn't change—intent eventually leads to results—thriving companies know that their focus along the way must be a steadfast commitment to the people who perform the actions that drive results. Sales and profits become outcomes, not targets.

ATTRIBUTE 2: THINK, PLAN, DO, MEASURE

Less than a year ago, an organization I work with faced a major crisis. One of their main products—a staple of their business—was facing a shortage due to elements outside of the company's control. The markets were highly volatile, cost of the product was up, and the whole situation was having a significant impact on the organization.

While other companies would have simply tried to stay afloat and later struggled to deal with the aftermath of the shortage, my client did something smart: The company faced the challenge head-on.

Leaders in the organization spent time thinking through the problem, then called an initiative team together and laid out a plan. They discussed and created accountability with each person involved in the team. Then, they acted. Each individual fulfilled his or her responsibility based on the plan they had put together. Along the way, they measured their effectiveness through their buy strategies, market positioning, manufacturing strategies and, the ultimate measure, profits.

That year, many publicly traded companies reported less-than-expected earnings. My clients finished with a record year.

There are four things my client did and did well: They thought, they planned, they did and they measured. As an owner or leader in a family company, that means you must think about your work, plan your work, do your work and measure your work. Think, plan, do, measure. What you can name through planning, you can measure; what you can measure, you can improve. When you don't see the results you want, make the appropriate adjustments.

It's a concept I refer to as simplex: complex idea, simple application. It's complex when you think about how the think-plan-do-measure method is applied across so many dimensions of a business. But it's the simplest of ideas that drives the concept. After all, thinking, planning, doing and measuring seem relatively straightforward, right? In concept, yes. In application, not necessarily.

The simplexity of this idea is represented in the way family businesses maximize their performance. They pride themselves on the simplicity of their business while still understanding the complexities needed to run that business. They don't want bureaucracies; if they did, they'd create bureaucratic companies. They don't want innately complex business structures that are too difficult for everyone in their organization to understand. They want to run an organization that is known for effectiveness.

The biggest detriment to family companies as they grow is not focusing on a limited and defined number of key measures.

Companies that aren't able to sustain profitability year after year continually chase after issues as they appear on the horizon. Measuring effectively begins with understanding the elements of useful metrics by looking at the patterns of your business objectively. Every measurement must be credible, accurate and valid. The results will provide insight into what has happened and what is likely to happen in the future. Reliable measurement provides the insight to understand needed changes and improvements to maximize performance.

Ask yourself, how often do I spend time purposefully thinking about challenges my company faces? How well does my organization plan? How well do we do? Can we measure what we've planned and done?

When I see a company maximizing, I can almost always pinpoint specific ways they've thought, planned, done and measured. They spent time thinking purposefully before planning, they established a well-thought-out plan, they executed that plan, and they measured to understand what worked, what didn't and what they needed to do next time.

I have a client and good friend who refers to the "sucker punch" of business: No matter how good you think you are, business will reach up, sucker punch you, and remind you that you're not that good. Usually, it's something you should have seen coming or prepared for, but it snuck up and leveled a blow nonetheless. It can hurt almost as much as someone punching you in the gut, though while your gut will feel better in minutes or hours, a sucker punch in business can take weeks, months or years to recover from.

The think-plan-do-measure method helps anticipate and avoid the sucker punch. It gets everybody in the organization on the same page. Each and every person in a company should follow a simple method: We think about the problem, we establish the plan, we do the work, and we measure the outcome.

ATTRIBUTE 3: DO THE RIGHT THING

If there is one mantra common among the majority of thriving family companies, it is this: Do the right thing.

This doesn't mean do the right thing while you consider other options. It doesn't mean do the right thing if it benefits your leadership agenda. It doesn't mean do the right thing as long as it doesn't impede your earnings. In businesses that aren't concerned about their legacy, doing the right thing has a qualifier, and that's where people get into trouble. Doing the right thing can't have a qualifier. You really have to put that statement to the test, because sometimes doing the right thing doesn't resonate with the things you'd like to do, even though it does connect with the things you have to do.

Doing the right thing can't have a qualifier.

When I reflect on this maxim, I'm reminded of a past client. There was a tragic accident at the company's plant, and an employee lost his life. The entire organization was devastated. No owner or leader ever wants to see someone die in the course of his job.

Sadly, the accident was a result of a compromise in process on the part of the employee. But that didn't matter to the leadership team—not at all. They could have justified who was or wasn't to blame, but that never happened. Instead, the client immediately engaged people. The company was quickly in touch with the family and offered to cover funeral costs, assist the family financially and fly in members of the family who did not live nearby. They looked for ways to help the family overcome the situation, both emotionally and financially, because they knew the family couldn't afford the cost burden to their household.

I suppose you could look at the situation and say, well, they were avoiding a lawsuit. But that was absolutely not what happened. They did it because it was the right thing to do. They treated people with dignity and respect. They recognized the loss of life. They acknowledged the loss to a family.

I've seen less traumatic examples too. Another client chose to recall a product before a recall was required. While it had a significant impact on their business in the short term, they wanted to have no question about the way they handled things. They said, "We will notify customers and communicate what's going on." Again, this wasn't because compliance mandated it but because, like other thriving family companies, their values and ethics compelled them to do the right thing.

As an owner or leader in a family business, you have that same opportunity. You get the chance to live your values. You are fortunate enough to have the freedom and flexibility to impact, develop, guide and lead people. Ask yourself, why do we do what we do? Your answer should be simple: because we get the opportunity to do the right thing.

ATTRIBUTE 4: CREATE THE EXPERIENCE

Have you ever been to Dutch Bros. Coffee? I went to one for the first time a few months back—and I wish I'd discovered it sooner. Now, I drive out of my way just to get coffee there. As someone used to big chain coffee, getting my morning coffee at Dutch Bros. is quite an experience.

First, the building itself is unique in appearance: bright blue roof, large images of a windmill (the Dutch Bros. logo) on the signage and building, a bright red and blue menu, and often a Dutch flag or two flying. It's not just a cookie-cutter structure that looks like every other coffee shop. Second, the prices all include tax, so I know exactly what I have to pay. Third, I'm greeted by a smiling, energetic barista who takes my coffee order without staring at a screen. When there are long lines, some locations will send someone to walk between cars and take orders—there's no impersonal voice box greeting you as you pull up. And finally, as my coffee is being made, the barista asks questions—how has my day been, what do I have planned, what was the coolest thing I did this past weekend, and more. As I leave, I'm enthusiastically wished a great day. The purpose? It's partially to distract me from the fact that making coffee can take a while. But it's also because the company has a solid culture focused around positivity and customer satisfaction. All of this adds up to a relentless pursuit of experience for me, the customer.

A privately held company, Dutch Bros. has focused on experience at every level of the organization, from the quality of coffee—every bean is roasted by hand in the Pacific Northwest—to the excellence of their employees. It's not surprising that in 2012, J.D. Power and Associates ranked the company as highest in customer satisfaction as compared to other coffee companies.[5]

Dutch Bros. demonstrates that a devotion to creating the optimal experience starts with a simple approach that says, "I value you." It all comes back to connectivity of relationship and communication. You may never be able to serve the customer perfectly, but you must see the customer as the reason for what you do, not an interruption.

As a family-owned business, you must make every aspect of your interaction with the customer about the experience. Never lose sight of the fact that you can create an experiential culture that is different from every other organization out there. You have advantages publicly held organizations don't: the ability to communicate effectively, make decisions rapidly, and get things done quicker without layers of bureaucracy. You can create a custom experience because of the freedom of being privately held. Never lose sight of that.

> **You must make every aspect of your interaction with the customer about the experience.**

ATTRIBUTE 5: BE RELENTLESSLY AWARE EXTERNALLY AND INTERNALLY

Is the emphasis of your company internally driven or externally driven? When I ask this question of new clients, the answer is almost always the same: externally driven. If that is your response, I'll ask a follow-up question: Do your actions support your answer?

Many times, it can be easy to become consumed by the bureaucracy or internal dynamics of an organization. One person may be arguing with another person about something that needs to be done, and meanwhile customers aren't getting what they need. Or there may be so many hoops to jump through that decisions aren't being made quickly enough to serve the customer. It becomes easy to forget that the customer is the reason for your existence. When this happens, actions become separated from a consideration for the customer.

In a family business, you have an opportunity to represent the customer in your actions. You get to transcend layers of bureaucracy that define what decisions "should be" or "must be," usually with no room for common sense or a true dedication to taking care of the customer. No, the customer isn't always right. No, you can't make every single decision based solely on the customer. But you can become externally driven by acting in a way that respects the customer as your reason for being. Much like when General Electric realized it needed to shed the "distractions" of nonessential business units, you have an opportunity to have an unrelenting focus on the people who make your company go 'round: your customers.

A client of mine illustrates this perfectly. The company is the hot dog supplier for a major-league baseball team, an organization with whom my client has had a long-term relationship. Each season, the stadium has a special "Dollar Dog Night" where you can get a hot dog for a buck. Several years back, people went crazy for hot dogs on Dollar Dog Night—and the stadium management quickly realized they were going to run out by the end of the evening. Baseball without hot dogs? In the MLB world, that would be a crisis.

A manager at the stadium made a call to the vice president of sales for my client. After the manager explained the situation, the vice president responded quickly. "No problem," he said. "We'll get people to the warehouse, we'll load the hot dogs, and we'll get them to you as quickly as we can."

The people in my client's company executed based on a commitment to their customer. They loaded the hot dogs into a refrigerated truck and drove them the sixty minutes to the stadium. The customer was happy, baseball fans were happy, and my client stayed true to their culture of creating the customer experience. This externally driven approach is what wins them awards and recognition for being a premier supplier.

As a family-owned business, you get to transcend the bureaucracy of a "big" organization. I'm using "big" as an attitude, not in relation to size. My client's company is big in traditional terms. But they have an attitude of service. They didn't allow their internal processes to hinder their response to external demands from the customer. Likewise, I encourage you to be relentlessly aware of both sides—internal and external—and how they impact your actions.

ATTRIBUTE 6: VIEW SITUATIONS OBJECTIVELY

I recently observed a colleague of mine from Kentucky, Ryan Lisk, conduct an exercise with a group of about fifty leaders. He began by telling the group their job was to pick the winner of an upcoming horse race. Initially, they were only given the horse's name and number and asked to pick the winner. He informed them he was going to later provide information in order to help them "handicap" the race.

After their initial selections, Ryan then introduced new information about the horses the group may have found useful: odds, jockey, trainer and even past performance data. It was all information that would impact the outcome of the race.

At each point, he paused and gave the audience the opportunity to "change their bets." And although the data he revealed was clearly pointing to the eventual winner of the race, guess how many people from the room of fifty actually changed their pick from the original horse they chose. Twenty? Fifteen? Ten? Not even. Just two people changed their picks. Ryan has done this exercise numerous times, and it's almost always the same scenario, with just a few people changing their minds once the facts are presented.

> Objectivity is a requirement because subjectivity and emotion are two defaults that can lead to bad decision-making.

I see similar situations occur in family businesses. Despite the information available, regardless of the data that can help leaders improve their odds and effectiveness in decision-making, they still go with what they believe to be correct. Instead of operating from their "gut" (subjective), they need to take a more logical approach (objective).

There is no place this is more prominent than with people. If you look at one dimension of a person, you know one thing. If you look at multiple dimensions of a person, you can understand her drives and motivations, what makes her most effective as a part of the organization, even if she is a good fit for the company at all. Unfortunately, leaders often fall in love with intuitiveness and forget the importance of facts and data, especially as they relate to people. And no, I'm not talking about reviewing work history and education; I'm referencing using assessments and tools to provide objective information about individuals.

Thriving family businesses know that objectivity is a requirement because subjectivity and emotion are two defaults that can lead to bad decision-making—especially when it comes to problems or challenges. To avoid this trap, they do the following:

1. Define and consider the problem rather than attacking a person. Too often, emphasis is placed on a person, and the problem that is being confronted isn't actually defined.

2. Gather as much information as possible from various sources to assist in working through the problem. Leaders must make sure the sources aren't representing their own agendas or creating bias.

3. Form an opinion and determine the appropriate course of action based on a defined problem.

Organizations that thrive function not from what they think they know. Instead, they make decisions from what they objectively know. They benchmark positions and define key accountabilities required for superior performance. They align people and positions as objectively as possible, given experience and background, cultural fit, and requirements and accountabilities of the position. They recognize that to grow and succeed, they must make choices based on good, sound information, not exclusively on opinions or intuition.

ATTRIBUTE 7: MAINTAIN AN ADVANCING PERSPECTIVE

I recently read a quote from an interview in *Bloomberg Business* that stuck with me: "Education is something that happens to you. Learning is something you do for yourself."[6] I keep coming back to that article because it resonates with me as someone who works with family companies. Too often, I see owners and leaders who are letting their businesses happen to them. They're not doing for themselves—learning, adapting and growing.

Thriving is a choice that is purposefully made and lived out by working *on* the business (active) rather than working solely *in* the business (passive). When passivity takes hold, the strengths that built the business can quickly become the factors that limit the business.

A perfect example is illustrated by one of my clients. The owners are the leading sales producers for the organization. This was a strength as they grew the business but is now becoming a limitation as they need to continue to advance the business. They must shift from working *in* the business to working *on* the business.

Often, owners forget they are the most important influencers of growth. But consider this:

What position has the primary responsibility and key accountability of defining and communicating the strategy of the business? The owner.

What position has the main responsibility of working on the company and defining strategic direction? The owner.

What position is often consumed by working in the business? The owner.

What position usually begins selling and continues to be the leading salesperson of the company's products and/or services? The owner.

What position, even with all of the right intent, can become the greatest limitation to further growing and maximizing the opportunities of the organization? You guessed it: the owner.

Even in successful organizations, one of the greatest limiters is moving the owners who have a clear understanding of what it means to work in the business (activity) to understanding the accountability of working on the business (strategy). They have also often been educated by a previous generation in what it means to grow the business (again, activity) but have failed to consider or learn for themselves what it means to maximize the business through a defined strategy.

When I talk about education versus learning, what I'm really talking about is stagnation versus advancing. I encourage you to maintain an advancing perspective because that's what will propel you forward. Owners who are maximizing their business—who are truly preserving love, legacy and leadership for generations to come—get that they must work *on* the business in addition to working *in* the business.

ATTRIBUTE 8: DEVELOP AND EXECUTE AN EVOLUTION PLAN

Earlier, I told the story of a leader I greatly admire who is intentionally spending four to five years transitioning his company to the next generation of leaders. His story is one I would encourage leaders of all organizations to emulate. He recognizes that the decades he's devoted to building the business and the people he's spent years molding for leadership are worth the effort to create a thorough evolution strategy.

Too often, I see family companies handed off haphazardly. And even more common, I see the "boomerang effect" of leaders who intend to redefine their roles, reduce their day-to-day involvement or retire but instead end up coming back around to clean up the mess they left upon their departure. Don't be that leader.

Evolving or transitioning a business is like walking a tightrope. On a tightrope, you start at one end and the purpose of your journey is to get to the other end. As you step onto the rope, you begin the delicate balancing act that you must continue flawlessly: holding a bar in your hands to help maintain balance, stepping along the thin line, and shifting your weight ever so slightly to keep from falling off. One wrong move, even if it's just the smallest misstep, can send you hurtling towards the ground.

In business, you also walk a tightrope, especially when it comes to evolving your business. The objective is to get from one point to another, or one generation to another, and not fall off. To do this well, you must be constantly aware of where you are and where you are going, and you must continually assess your position.

The objective is that eventually, with work and time, you create enough stability in your organization that the tightrope becomes a footbridge. When you make it a footbridge, you now get the opportunity to make it a two-lane bridge, and when you've done that and are really moving to a place of thriving, it becomes a four-lane bridge. With each careful step, each correct decision, you give yourself more space and there is less volatility as you continue to evolve. The bridge becomes a secure space that new leaders can cross, step by step, as they take over leadership and continue the thriving mindset for years to come.

A solid plan is your best defense against losing your footing in the delicate process that is evolution or transition. If you want to adopt a thriving mindset, you must look to the future. You must develop and execute a plan.

ATTRIBUTE 9: MAINTAIN THE HEART

I'm going to ask you an important question. I want you to consider this question and answer it as honestly as possible. Be truthful, because your response can reveal a lot about where you are and where you're headed as a family company owner or leader. Ready? Here it is.

Do you still want to love your family—son, daughter, cousin, niece, uncle, whoever it may be—when you're done working through the challenges and maximizing the opportunities in your company?

Think about it for a moment then answer a simple yes or no. Leave out any qualifiers.

I once asked this question of leaders in a company I was helping transition from second-generation brothers to their children. The son of one brother and the daughter of the other brother were both in vice president roles, and the daughter was promoted to president, leaving the son angry and irritated. A chasm formed between the cousins. The son wasn't fit to lead, and though the daughter had potential, the complexity of the situation and the company left her in a position with limited choices. Before I moved forward with my recommendations, I asked this simple question to the cousins: Do you care if you love each other when we're done with this process?

> **Family businesses that thrive have one important commonality: Family members love each other.**

Each answered simply: no. In that moment, I learned an important lesson about working with the leaders of family companies. Just like you can't pass on motivation to someone else, you can't impart the desire or intent to preserve the love, legacy and leadership of a family in business together. They must want to maintain their own heart. In all my years working with family businesses, I have only seen a situation like that twice. It was hard for everyone, and as an impartial advisor looking on, I could predict the future with near certainty. Eventually, they sold their company, which was the correct decision for all involved.

Family businesses that thrive have one important commonality: Family members love each other.

They can disagree. They can dislike each other at times. But at the end of the day, they still maintain their heart for each other. Family members have to care and want to preserve their relationships while growing their company. It's a prerequisite to the continuity of love, legacy and leadership.

As family members move through communication challenges, at the center of their heart for each other is the principle of "our." Seeing the family and leadership team as a unit is critical. There aren't "your" decisions or "my" decisions; there are only *our* decisions. It wasn't your dad's decision or your daughter's decision; it was all of yours. Own the fact that, as leaders in your organization, you work as a unit. Maintain that solidarity, heart and respect for generations past, present and future.

And finally, maintaining the heart doesn't mean being blind. Even though you love your relatives, you must be able to recognize reality. Strive to see things how they really are, not as you wish them to be. Separate delusion from reality. Work to move past what you think you know to be able to objectively know what's going on in your organization.

But do so recognizing that even if your objective approach reveals deficiencies or limitations in the people you love, that's OK. You can still love your family. Maintaining your heart for each other is perhaps the most important thing you can do to help your family business thrive.

SUMMING UP

Adopting a thriving mindset is work. Thriving requires belief: in abundance ahead of scarcity, in the pursuit of something that cannot yet be fully seen or completely understood. A thriving mindset challenges each leader to move towards an outcome of perseverance. It requires steadfastness and maturity to stay the course towards completion.

We've discussed nine attributes of family companies with this mindset. To review, they are the following:

1. See sales and profits as outcomes, not targets.

2. Think, plan, do, measure.

3. Do the right thing.

4. Create the experience.

5. Be relentlessly aware externally and internally.

6. View situations objectively.

7. Maintain an advancing perspective.

8. Develop and execute an evolution plan.

9. Maintain the heart.

Adopting all nine of these attributes takes intentional, dedicated work over years. In fact, the work never really stops because you must—*must*—maintain that intentionality, the relentless pursuit of excellence, each and every day. If you find yourself falling short in one or several of these areas, it's time to objectively evaluate where you are and where you're headed. Doing so with the assistance of an outside advisor is key in helping assess where you are currently, so you can develop a plan of moving forward.

Do you notice something important absent from the list of nine attributes? If you thought "culture," you're absolutely right. That's because the topic deserves additional exploration and space. We'll start with the story of an old oak tree.

4

Creating the Culture

On the property of a large, family-owned organization resides an old oak tree. Its wide trunk and sprawling crown could tell stories of the four generations of leaders who have sat under its branches. The great tree's roots extend deep into the ground, anchoring itself in the history of the company and its culture, making the oak as much a part of the organization as the building and people, the processes and procedures that have helped this organization become one of the just 3 percent of companies that survive into the fourth generation.

Decades ago, the company was still run by the second-generation owner who knew his son would someday take over the company. He eagerly anticipated beginning the transition process, but he didn't plan on waiting until he was ready to retire. Instead, it would begin when his son turned thirteen. In this family, thirteen was a special age not just because a child entered his teen years but because he was old enough to begin transitioning into the family business.

When this owner's son came of age, the two began what became a weekly "meeting" under that old oak. They would bring their lunches and spend an hour beneath the tree every week without fail. The father would talk to his son about family, responsibility and the culture of the company. The son would listen intently, trying his best to understand the wisdom his father shared, knowing that someday, years down the road, he would be taking his father's place. The boy knew, too, that he would bring his own future child to the oak tree and teach the same principles that had been passed down for generations.

Sadly, the two did not get as many years together as they had hoped. When the son was in his early thirties, the father was diagnosed with an aggressive disease. The father passed not long after, leaving a cultural legacy that the son knew was his responsibility to continue.

Culture, in this case, was about the continuity of a conversation between a father and son. Those nineteen years of conversations centered on the balanced approach the son needed in his view of life. And that son—now a grown man who has been running a multimillion-dollar organization for more than forty years—has taken the same approach with his son through a continuity of conversation, but he's done so with even greater deliberateness and urgency because he realizes time is finite.

ENCULTURATION

The owner of this company has focused on what is known as "enculturation," or the immersion of an individual into a culture of a family and organization. It's a way of creating an awareness of the culture. I've watched the same dynamic occur in other ways: walks around the office, weekly lunches, regular phone calls. It doesn't matter how it's done but rather *that* it's done. These conversations transcend the business; they cover the physical, mental and spiritual. Topics of discussion include people, processes and customers. They are dialogues about both business and values. It's all about imparting balance: business in balance, life in balance, thoughts in balance.

This is a highly personal approach to business—an approach that only makes sense in the family structure. Such a transfer of information becomes critical early on, not later when the owner is ready to exit the company.

If the second-generation owner were still alive today, he would be proud of the cultural legacy he passed to his son and the continuance of that legacy through his grandson. That culture has transcended his death and has continued to breathe life into the organization and family for which he cared so deeply. He was wise enough to know that the transition of cultural values—deliberate enculturation of his son—needed to begin early and continue not for years but for decades.

Some might criticize enculturation as being too idealistic. I disagree. Creating a broad and deep awareness by immersing someone into an organization's culture cannot be done quickly. It must be done intentionally over time.

While the son's choices have been his own as he has run the company, the enculturation he experienced from those conversations with his father have remained a part of him. This has created roots so deep that no one can uproot them—like the oak tree on the company's property, the culture of the organization will endure as long as the conversation continues.

Here's what's key too: that culture extends to the entire organization. The tree's roots sprawl outward. They metaphorically spread throughout the company and even reach customers. Every leader, every employee, can tell you what it means to be a part of that company. They may use different words, but they know what the culture is: how they view people and processes, how they approach differentiation in the marketplace, how they maintain an attitude of resourcefulness. Because four generations of leaders have not only focused on enculturation of their children but also of the leaders of the company, it becomes glaringly obvious when someone doesn't fit the cultural dynamic.

Culture, then, becomes a uniting force within a company, one that ties everyone together into a single mindset: one of thriving.

WHAT IS CULTURE?

The word "culture" has become such a buzzword these days that its meaning has become diluted. We could go with Merriam-Webster's version: "a way of thinking, behaving, or working that exists in a place or organization (such as a business)."[1] But I'll offer a slightly different version: the distinct way in which an organization thinks, does and functions.

More so, culture is the passing on of stories. It's a strong work ethic. It's describing and living out one's values. It's the desire and intent to do the right thing. It's valuing achievement but not becoming so consumed by it that accomplishments are about "me" rather than "we." It's understanding confidence and humility as a necessary blend in leadership style. It's recognizing, as a leader, that you can't become too full of yourself because you'll become awfully unfulfilled in what matters. It's the total of all that impacts the spirit, people, performance and profitability of your company. Those are the dynamics of culture.

Another thing I've found, almost across the board, is that if you have a strong cultural connection in your own life, you have an easier time connecting to the culture of an organization. Helping organizations define culture is a natural process for me for the simple fact that I have a strong cultural heritage within my own family and upbringing.

From the time I can remember our conversations, my dad has talked to me about the importance of living below one's means and avoiding incurring debt. My mom and dad have both emphasized humility in philanthropy, giving not for recognition but because of a dedication to serving others above yourself. A strong cultural upbringing has, in part, allowed me to help others recognize and define culture in their own lives and organizations.

Of course, that's not to say that those who didn't have great parental figures growing up are doomed. You can connect to culture in a number of ways—through family, through community, through a personal dedication to public service, through a religious devotion.

And to add to that, every family, community and organization *does* have a culture. Good or bad, that culture exists. In a company, the organization takes on the characteristics of its leader. Are you a leader who makes everyone feel included and part of the purpose of the company? The likelihood is that your employees behave similarly. Are you more focused on the bottom line than in the happiness of your staff? Your people are probably centered on figures more than on team and personal development. As an owner,

Culture is the distinct way in which an organization thinks, does and functions.

as a leader, your example—the culture you create—sets the tone of the entire company. It determines the distinct way the people in your organization think, do and function.

The best example I can think of is a long-standing client of mine. Every single week, the owner, president, vice president of sales, director of HR, and other leaders walk their facilities. As their business advisor, the expectation is that I will walk through their facilities and gain firsthand awareness and perspective, as well. These leaders interact with the employees, the people who keep the company running day in and day out. It's a cultural norm. They go to the heart of where things are produced to learn about, understand and consider the employees. They don't sit in an office and believe they can impart wisdom to people; they recognize the importance of creating a culture of respect. And let me tell you, that cultural norm has spread throughout the entire organization, all the way to the newest employee.

As the owner or leader of a family company, you, too, have the opportunity to run your organization in a way that values culture. In many publicly traded companies, culture cannot be entirely valued because regulations are so fully defined that they get in the way of the organization defining a truly differentiated culture. You have a choice to define culture, live it out and watch it spread through your organization like the sprawling roots of a decades-old oak. Everyone has the opportunity to act in a way that connects to culture. Will you make that choice? Will you lead by example and with awareness? Will you sit under oak trees, walk your facilities, and listen to your people? That's how great cultures—and talent—are developed.

THE FIVE FOUNDATIONS OF CULTURE

There are five foundations of culture I've found to be common across family companies: clarity, communication, collaboration, cooperation and respect. These foundations are so universal that they extend beyond business walls and impact relationships. Leaders have told me how understanding these five foundations has improved their family relationships, friendships and even marriages.

Clarifying culture, dealing with communication, establishing collaboration and cooperation, and creating an environment of respect set in motion an opportunity for performance shifts. And from small shifts emerge an evolution to thriving by preserving the love, legacy and leadership of your family company.

CLARITY

Imagine that you wear reading glasses to correct poor, near-sighted vision. You're sitting next to a woman who also wears corrective lenses to read but uses a completely different prescription. You each remove your glasses and hand them to the other person; you put on the woman's glasses as she puts on yours. I hand you a piece of paper and ask you to read it, but all you see is a blur, what looks like fuzzy, black ink blotches on the page. I then ask if you have at least a feel for what it says. You say no. Of course you can't—you can't see it at all.

Then, I ask you to switch glasses back so you once again have your correct prescription. I request that you read the page, and this time, it's clear. You know exactly what it says. There is no confusion.

It's the same with clarity of culture. Everyone—*everyone*—in your organization must be aware of the culture. It must be clearly defined. Every level of team member must know it intimately. That clarity influences how people think, plan, do and measure.

> **A lack of focus around culture creates a lack of focus elsewhere in the company too. Clarity of culture positively influences the performance of your business.**

If culture is fuzzy, if it's cloudy, if people in the organization can't understand it because they can't see it being lived out by you, the leader, there is no clarity. There is a lack of focus. And a lack of focus around culture creates a lack of focus elsewhere in the company too. Clarity of culture positively influences the performance of your business. This means that when confronted with a decision or choice, people within the company know what they do, why they do it, when to do it, who they are doing it for, and how it is to be done.

Clarity is absolutely number one. There's a reason it's first in my list of five—the culture must be clear for the four other foundations to exist.

COMMUNICATION

Communication is the foundation to defining cultural clarity and expectations and having people translate that definition into actions. Communication is not simply talking, and it's not simply listening or a combination of the two—it's understanding another person as definably unique and truly desiring to connect. Part of establishing solid communication is understanding people objectively. Many organizations take a strictly intuitive approach, but that's not enough.

If I could work with every family company in the United States today and do only one thing, it would be to help them quantifiably understand every person in their organization: how they do what they do, why they do what they do, their awareness and insight, and the skills they possess and demonstrate, along with their emotional quotient (the ability to sense, understand and effectively apply the power of emotions to facilitate higher levels of collaboration and productivity). I would do this for a single reason, and that is because it would allow people to communicate with others in a uniquely individual and most effective way. How do I help clients quantifiably understand their people? Through the use of validated and objective assessment resources.

At this point, you might be thinking, "I'm a leader. Of course I communicate." Nonsense. Just because you're a leader and just because you say things to people doesn't mean you're communicating with them. Unless you've taken the time to objectively understand each person on your team and sincerely desire to connect, you have not moved past talking into true communication.

If you want to communicate with someone, a good place to start is through understanding and awareness. Assessments provide predictive insight and give you perspective on an individual's behaviors and driving forces. They help answer questions like:

- How do you like to make decisions?

- How do you like to interact with people?

- Are you more realistic or optimistic? Aggressive or reflective?

- How do you prefer to handle the pace of your environment?

- Do you like a frenetic, go-get-it, always-urgent dynamic, or do you prefer a more deliberate methodology?

- How do you like to deal with rules and structure?

- Why do you like to do what you do? What gets you out of bed in the morning and showing up for work every day?

If you don't know how someone prefers to do things, how are you ever going to communicate effectively? Understanding people objectively helps build a picture that allows you to figure out how you can best interact with them. You aren't just basing it off what you think you know; you're combining it with what you actually know about a person, on a measured and assessed basis. The predictability of an individual matters, not in that their actions are always predictable but in knowing, "Here's how I need to approach you."

Really understanding how to communicate with others is the hardest and most rewarding work you will ever do as a leader. It doesn't seem to connect to the tasks or processes of the business, and therefore it's often viewed as less essential or less important. But it's far from unimportant. Clarity combined with communication brings about a powerful differentiated advantage around people.

COLLABORATION

Imagine sitting silently and alone among a roomful of people. There is no one to bounce ideas off of or share insights with, even though you're surrounded by a crowd. You leave only with the ideas you came with, having gained no collaborative or external perspective. This scenario isn't far from reality in many organizations.

A lack of collaboration is a genuine problem facing people and companies alike. In so many ways, individuals can't get past the words and directives to really understand what it means to work together. Conversely, when they try to collaborate on everything, they can wind up in endless meetings, debating

> **Really understanding how to communicate with others is the hardest and most rewarding work you will ever do as a leader.**

ideas and struggling to find the real benefit of collaboration.

There are two components to miserable collaboration: lacking awareness of how someone communicates and constantly judging why a person does things. So many times in a family company setting, "not liking someone" gets in the way of collaborating with that person.

Some of the best conversations I have with leaders to help advance their culture centers around confronting judgment. We work together to identify areas where leaders are judging others within an organization simply because another's view is not exactly the same. I help these leaders sort out what it really means to communicate and collaborate in a practical sense that is directly related to the performance outcomes and results of their business.

When considering collaborating with others, I have a very simple rule. Let's assume there are two people who want to learn to communicate better together; they really are trying to understand the other person at an objective level. Jane wants to talk to Tom about a matter that is taking place within the company, and she approaches Tom to do so. In this case, Jane has the obligation to consider Tom—his personality, drives, insights, all of which have already been measured objectively. That doesn't let Tom off the hook for collaborating, but it does give responsibility to the person who initiates the discussion to focus on fostering collaboration.

Now, say Tom has a topic to discuss with Jane. He approaches her. He is then obligated to consider her perspective. Likewise, if you go to others, you consider them; if they come to you, they consider you. I call it the rules of engagement, and they have served well to help organizations work on their collaboration and communication. And as collaboration is strengthened, so is the company's culture.

Think of a collaborative culture as a by-product or measure of individuals who are:

- Passionately curious. They crave new insights and want to talk with people who have different perspectives. Such individuals don't presume or believe that they have all the answers. They can connect the dots.

- Modestly or humbly confident. They bounce ideas off of others without turning it into a competition or validation of their expertise. These people create a lot of "what if" scenarios.

- Reasonably obsessed. They care more about the collective mission than about how achieving goals will benefit their personal fortunes.

The best companies have leaders who are part of a "collaboration community." Leadership cultivates and contributes ideas with an awareness of value, trust and flow rather than supreme intelligence, expertise or credibility. They seek out colleagues they don't know or automatically relate with and understand individual styles by observing, listening and contributing. They are on the lookout for knowledge others possess that they can benefit from.

True collaboration extends to the practicality of decisively transforming the performance capacity of people and companies to achieve a distinct competitive advantage. Collaborating ignites the deep need each of us has to be a part of a defined purpose, strategy and direction.

COOPERATION

There is a lot of talk in the business world about breaking down silos. The term "silo" refers to a mindset of maintaining departmental barriers and withholding information between different areas in the company. This can translate to people on an individual level too—not wanting to share and co-operate with others.

> **The trouble with the trendy focus on breaking down silos is that there is little focus on how.**

The trouble with the trendy focus on breaking down silos is that there is little focus on how. Cooperation, quite simply, is the elimination of communication or collaboration barriers within an organization—the elimination of silos. The most important thing is how we break those silos down: individually assessing and understanding each person as an individual; collectively understanding the organization as a whole based on these individuals; looking at the human dynamic that is contributing to business performance; and evaluating the level of cooperation that actually exists.

If your organization has people with similar values and considerations for why they do things, even if they have different behaviors, what will you have? Greater cooperation. If your organization has individuals with little to no alignment in values and different ways of communicating, what will you have? In some cases, almost no cooperation.

Understanding why your organization is—or isn't—cooperating *must* begin with an understanding of people.

One way I help organizations cooperate better is by helping them establish a common language, a result of the quantifiable assessments I do with individuals. People then have terminology that helps describe themselves and others; they can explain what they intuitively feel. They understand what's being communicated under the oak tree, but more importantly, they understand who they are and who the other person under the oak tree is. All the common language does is bring an awareness of what someone already feels, knows and maybe even understands about themselves—they just haven't been able to name it.

My role as an advisor in this area is clearly defined. I help people identify and eliminate barriers to establish cooperation that advances the organization. And this company-wide emphasis of awareness becomes part of the cultural foundations of the organization.

RESPECT

How can you begin to communicate with respect? You come to greater levels of understanding. You value others for their role and expertise. You see them as the "go-to" people and seek them out to gain their insight and perspective. Respect is the approach and the outcome.

Disrespect in a company is like waves pounding against the shore, slowly, consistently creating erosion. That's why a culture of disrespect must be viewed as a problem. If it's allowed to exist, it will consistently lead to the erosion of communication, collaboration and cooperation.

If you're backtracking from a lack of respect within your organization, start with an awareness of people. As I've said before, things may get worse before they get better. You must treat the situation, the dysfunction of a culture of disrespect, as a problem. People must confront themselves with who they are, not who they think they are. They must first understand themselves, then understand everybody else, and then start working on all of the elements that need to be addressed to get the factors of clarity, communication, collaboration, cooperation and respect established.

Notice that I, once again, list clarity first. To have a culture of respect, you must have clarity, and that starts with a clear understanding of people. When people begin to understand themselves and others, it creates greater clarity. From that clarity emerges different communication. And from that different communication, respect. There's your shift; there's your chance. That's how you start to move a culture in a different, better direction.

CLEARLY DEFINING YOUR CULTURE

As you work to adopt a thriving mindset, one of the most important things you can do is define your culture. Let's go back to the definition of culture: the distinct way in which an organization thinks, does and functions. As you begin this process, ask yourself,

- Have I defined how my organization thinks, does and functions?

- Have I written this definition down?

- Have I started teaching other people about the culture?

When I walk organizations through this process, it typically happens in three sessions. My role, which is a role I love, is strictly to facilitate thoughts in an organized way. First, I listen, and after I listen, I help these leaders work through a process of awareness, understanding, alignment and advancing.

Leaders must start by developing an awareness of what's important in their organizations. Next, they must understand where there are differences or disconnects. Then, they must identify where there are both differences and alignments around their responses in relation to the culture we've defined together. It's an interesting dialogue because it requires people to confront situations in which their thoughts, words and actions haven't aligned.

> **Leaders must develop an awareness of what's important in their organizations.**

After that, I help them advance the culture. We determine strategies to carry the culture into the workforce. To do this, they must have a clearly defined, concise cultural understanding summarized in a written statement. This cultural statement becomes the lifeblood of the organization, the thing that runs through all levels of leadership, an attitude and approach to business that are none other than the roots that anchor the company firmly in culture.

Once you define that culture and advance it into your organization, people begin connecting with it and becoming excited about it.

To help you begin to define the culture in your organization, you can start with an activity I use in my work with leaders. I suggest having each person on your leadership team complete this exercise as well, so you can begin to identify alignments and disconnects in your understanding of the company culture. It's best to involve an outside advisor in this process, but you can begin to gain insights even before you bring that person in. To complete the activity, write your answers to these questions and statements as entirely as possible:

1. Give five words that describe the values of your organization (e.g., integrity).

2. What do you see as the benefit and outcome of defining your company values and guiding principles?

3. List three to five elements of your company culture that are nonnegotiable in your mind.

4. In your opinion, what is at the core/foundation of your organization's success?

5. Describe how you see your role as it relates to the people of your company.

6. What are the top three ways in which your organization differentiates itself in the marketplace? Please be specific and list in order of importance.

7. From your perspective, is profit a target or an outcome? Should profit be achieved at the expense of a guiding principle or value? Please give details about your answers.

8. Based on your experience at your company, put the following statements in order of priority from 1 to 4 with 1 being of highest importance.

   - Our strategies

   - Our customers

   - Our values/principles

   - Our people

9. Why do customers buy from your company, and what makes your organization great?

10. Using only a few key words, please describe your company's culture.

After completing these questions, the next step is typically a series of conversations guided by an outside advisor. Those conversations lead to a clear, defined cultural statement. This is not a quick process, and it's not always easy to arrive at a clearly defined cultural statement when there are many differing opinions and personalities weighing in on the discussion. But it is worth the process. Once the company's culture is clearly defined, it can be shared throughout every level of the organization. It becomes the way of things—the central statement that guides every decision and action, how leaders and employees think, do, function and assess. It deepens the roots of the organization and aids in anchoring the cultural legacy of the company for generations to come.

THE MANY HATS YOU WEAR

Imagine that you have four hats sitting in front of you: a baseball hat, a cowboy hat, a football helmet and a construction hard hat. First, you put on the baseball hat; you're ready for a ball game. Next, you remove that hat and put on the cowboy hat; you're up for going horseback riding. Then, you take the cowboy hat off and replace it with the helmet; now you're suited up for a game of football. And finally, you remove the helmet and replace it with the hard hat; you're prepared and protected for construction work. Each swap happens quickly, and as you change hats, you metaphorically change roles, preparing yourself for a different task.

It's a similar situation in a family business. You are one person, but the hat you wear depends on the role of the moment. At any given time, and often within the same day or even a span of hours or minutes, you must be able and ready to switch roles and provide the appropriate response. You might be running part of the organization and need to deal with the functional day-to-day responsibilities of that role; you might sit on the board and need to consider the bigger picture from a board member's perspective; you might be a shareholder and need to consider your financial interest; and you might have a family challenge that requires you to deal with the issue at the level of relationship. Those are just four of the hats you likely wear: positional leader, board member, shareholder, family member. If you get confused about which hat you're wearing at what time, it can cause a host of issues.

Many times, people also identify with one hat, or role, as primary. This is the hat they are most comfortable in and most readily wear. It represents the path of least resistance and, in many cases, where they feel their greatest affinity.

I was once involved in a board meeting where the majority of the board was made up of family members, some who were positional leaders in the company and some who were not. To make this even more interesting, the family members came from separate households. Picture the game show *Family Feud* with two sides competing. Now imagine the game show goes haywire, and you can visualize what happened at the board meeting.

Family members involved with the business and on the board worked to maintain objectivity and connect decisions objectively to what was in the best interest of the company. They did a fine job of separating themselves from their positional roles/hats and clearly understood the hat they needed to wear. The family members who wore family member, shareholder and board member hats were more interested in fulfilling their individual preferences than making good decisions to positively impact the performance of the company.

Silly, I know, but this is what happens when preferences (subjective) are placed ahead of sound business strategy (objective). The outcome is a variety of nonessentials that are a complete distraction to the business. Family owners and leaders cannot elevate preferences above purpose.

> **Family owners and leaders cannot elevate preferences above purpose.**

The host—or better named, referee—of the show was, you guessed it, yours truly. I was there at the request of the owner and two external non-family board members to observe and gain insight ahead of the meeting. They wanted to talk with me about how evolving their company into the future could be different than how they had built it to this point.

The two external board members sat almost as observers themselves, only because to get a word in edgewise was nearly impossible. They understood their roles, and they were both fully capable and competent to serve on the board. To this point, the company had been successful in spite of itself, and the owner recognized that while they were posting great numbers, they weren't healthy, thriving, or in a position to maximize the love, legacy and leadership for future generations.

Like my client, you can make big strides in your effectiveness simply by recognizing three things: (1) how many hats exist, (2) how many hats you are responsible for wearing, and (3) which hat to wear (and when) to avoid confusion or chaos. Building this awareness can help you mentally transition when situations arise that require a hat switch—and create more harmony and success in the interactions you have with others.

What does this have to do with culture? As a leader, culture starts with you. What you do, what you say, and how you say and do it have ripple effects within your company. Often, the hat you are wearing influences how you deal with a situation. If you don't understand what hat to wear, how can you be the most effective cultural example for your organization? When this uncertainty arises, so do functional dysfunction and a resulting culture of confusion and, most likely, negativity.

Lack of clarity around how each of your definably unique roles all intertwine can lead to confusion. Confusion among leaders results in chaos. Chaos diminishes performance. When people don't know what hat they are to wear and in what situation, they tend to fight for preferences that don't support unity in terms of clarity, communication, collaboration, cooperation and respect. There's a distinct difference between a role, a preference and a family value. Preferences ahead of values, clarity, purpose and a clearly defined strategy result in entitlement, division and a lack of unity.

Cultural clarity starts with an objective understanding of yourself: how you do things, why you do things a certain way, and how and why you communicate the way you do. Then, you must define and understand the many hats you wear. You might need to acknowledge where your capacity to wear a hat is lacking and where your strongest capacity lies. You might need to recognize that you are not fully competent in an area and need to better understand the organization's needs and define the hats you must wear from here on out. Or you might need to assess the gaps in your competencies and decide whether you should pass a hat to someone else or take advantage of development opportunities. As an advisor, my role is to help owners and leaders identify the many hats in an organization and understand which hats need to be put on and which need to be taken off.

As you're changing hats, remember you're also walking that tightrope we explored earlier, always balancing decisions as you move forward in leading your company to a place of thriving. This changing of hats, this balancing act, goes on every day in the family company. And it will continue, from generation to generation, as long as the company remains.

PASSING ON THE CULTURAL LEGACY

In 1905, a safe was cast out of steel and iron. That safe accompanied a corporate attorney for Retail Credit Company, known today as Equifax, as he made regular trips between the northern United States and Arizona. The fireproof box held important papers the attorney needed while traveling, documents that required the utmost security. There could be no risk of being damaged, lost or stolen. For decades, that safe traveled alongside the attorney, protecting the information of people around the country.

On top of the safe was a name: Emory J. Hyde. My great-grandfather.

For generations, that safe has made its way through my family: to my grandmother and grandfather, his daughter and son-in-law; and then his grandson, my father. In each case, the safe was passed to the next generation by choice, not because of death—the older generation decided it was time to pass it on.

In order to receive the safe, there was and still is a requirement. You have to be able to open it. Since it was made in the early 1900s, the safe is based on a dial, and you have to turn it carefully and listen for the click as the pins are falling. You can't treat it like today's lock dials, which are imprecise. Make the slightest mistake, and you won't be able to open the safe.

One Saturday, my dad called me over to his house. When I arrived, he took me out to the garage. Sitting there was the safe.

"It's time to pass the safe on," he told me. "You know the legacy of this safe, and you know the stipulation—you have to be able to open it. No pressure, but think carefully as you're opening it. Here's the combination." He handed me a piece of paper and added that I wasn't allowed to touch the safe before beginning.

> **This changing of hats, this balancing act, goes on every day in the family company.**

In fact, I'd never been allowed to touch it while growing up. I had just one opportunity to open it, and if I failed, I'd have to wait for my next chance. And there was no telling when that would be.

I stared at the steel and iron box then down at the directions in my hands. I was already sweating; it was about 110 degrees outside in the dry Arizona heat, and there I was in an even hotter garage, about to become part of a legacy—or at least try to.

"Do I get any additional instructions?" I asked, looking at my dad.

"Nope. It's all there."

With a deep breath, I read the directions once more. Then I carefully, deliberately and purposefully began, imitating the way I'd seen my dad unlock it as I was growing up. I heard a click. I turned the dial back and heard another click. Then, I remembered my dad saying once that you have to be really careful when you hit the last number because once the pin falls, you have to carry the dial a little past. As I turned the dial to the last number, I heard the final click and carried it a little past, knowing that if I went too far, the safe wouldn't open.

My shirt was soaked with sweat, not just because it was hot but because I could feel the pressure of legacy and culture. It swelled in my head. I grabbed the handle of the safe and thought, please twist.

I twisted it carefully and the door opened. One try. I did it.

I turned towards my dad, and I could see the pride in his face. He said, "The safe is yours, and you can carry on the legacy to Bryce someday." I thought of my son and what it would be like passing the safe on to him. It was more than a steel and iron box at that moment; it was the history of my family, the passing on of a legacy that will continue well beyond when I pass from this earth.

Culture, the way the people in an organization think, do and function, is defined in moments like the one in my dad's garage. It's solidified under oak trees. It's established through deliberate conversations that span years, even decades. It's an awareness and value of what's truly unique.

As a part of a family company, you are part of something you have a responsibility to continue, something that comes with measurable accountability. When you influence others as a leader, you have to make sure they know that the culture of your family business matters. Decisions must be made based on more than the corporate balance sheet. As your people watch you make choices over the years based on culture, not just on quarterly or annual numbers, they will become motivated to do anything within reason to support the growth of the organization.

But first and foremost, you must recognize that you are not only part of a cultural legacy but a continuous contributor to its development.

You might already be responsible for the transition of that cultural legacy. You might be on the receiving end, like I was with the safe, like the boy was under the oak tree, of developing your own awareness of the legacy. No matter your status in the building and transferring of culture, you have a responsibility to yourself and your company to embrace and further the culture of your organization. Take the first step by building your awareness of culture and defining it. Then, take responsibility. Start inward. Like the roots of an oak tree, that inward understanding will spread through your actions and decisions, reaching out and out until every aspect of your organization is impacted for the better.

5

Letting Go

When was the last time you watched children at play? To kids, the world is open and new. There is nothing hindering their curiosity. They move through the world whimsically, creatively and innocently. They don't know boundaries or rules in most cases, particularly if they are in an environment where they can just be themselves.

Put a child in a room with a box of objects she has never seen before, and you'll see this creativity really blossom. She might struggle with an object at first, unsure of what to do with it. She'll draw from past experiences to try out a new item and experiment with play. Since she doesn't know its function, she might find a new use—one that, as adults, we would never have considered. A bowl might become a hat; a pom-pom might become an animal tail.

She is a blank canvas of the mind. She is open to the possibilities of what can be.

That pure and simple approach, that blank canvas, is what I want for you as a leader. I want you to learn to let go of what you think you know so you can thrive and advance on what you objectively know. I want you to have the creative openness of a child.

We can extend the concept of the blank canvas to artists too. An artist stands in front of his canvas, envisioning what can be. In the early stages, he is simply assessing what he might put on the white surface: a still life? a landscape? a portrait? There is endless possibility. Like a child approaching a box of new playthings, an artist gets the chance to play from a place of pureness.

Eventually, the artist decides what he will attempt to paint on his canvas. He might do a few initial sketches to consider the possibilities before ever placing a dot of paint. When he's ready—when he's thought through what can be—he begins to fill in the picture based on what is in front of him and what is in his mind.

Like children and artists, successful leaders start with a blank canvas of the mind and a clean slate from which to envision new ideas and consider alternative approaches. These leaders are adept at creatively assessing their problems so they can begin to paint their solutions. They don't let a head full of knowledge hinder creativity, but they do know when to pull from the past to help them approach challenges.

For the child, for the artist, for the leader, it's about creativity and openness.

When did you last spend time really thinking creatively about your business? How have you recently and tangibly started to consider something differently? Have you approached a problem with the same deliberate consideration of an artist, assessing what can be? Or has your default been to look to what you know and draw on the solutions that have worked in the past?

My hope is that you will start to explore what can be. To do so, you must start by letting go.

EXERCISING A DIFFERENT MINDSET

I owned the same elliptical for fourteen years. It was a good machine; it had never failed me. I'd gotten a solid workout on it and maintained a steady level of fitness for all those years. Yet while the elliptical did what I wanted it to do, I was getting bored. The workout was getting redundant. I noticed I wasn't pushing myself as hard because I was going into auto mode. One day after a particularly uninspiring workout, I thought to myself, when was the last time I considered the same exercise differently?

In fourteen years, I hadn't once—not once—considered buying a new machine. This thing *worked*, right? It was steadfast. It had never broken down, and it didn't seem like it would anytime in the near future.

In business, perhaps you've experienced something similar. You might have an idea or process that has been in place for years or a strategy that has been passed down from the previous generation of leadership. This way of thinking or doing has never failed you, not once in all that time, so why change things? You might feel like you're thriving because things are going smoothly and you're able to achieve the results you want.

But you don't really know if your idea, process or strategy is the best option unless you look at alternative options and consider fresh perspectives. For me, it was the simple act of going shopping for a new elliptical that opened up possibilities. I wasn't planning on buying; I was

> **You don't really know if your idea, process or strategy is the best option unless you look at alternative options and consider fresh perspectives.**

just looking. But as I began to see what was out there, I started seeing a whole new world of workouts open to me, not because mine was bad but because technology had advanced and improved.

Likewise, consider what you might find if you go "shopping." If you consider the value of your current mindset and methodologies in comparison to the return and value of new ideas and perspectives, you might find that you could be doing more than just moving through the motions every day. You could be thriving and finding new joy in doing so.

In his book, *Stop Selling Vanilla Ice Cream,* my friend and colleague Steve Van Remortel reflects that if everyone were content to eat vanilla ice cream, Baskin-Robbins® never would have created its thirty-one flavors marketing concept, offering a different flavor for every day of the month. He goes on to say that while vanilla remains the company's top-selling flavor, Burt Baskin and Irv Robbins realized early on that they couldn't just sell vanilla ice cream and hope to enjoy long-term success. Van Remortel's point is that no company can stop selling their vanilla, but every organization must differentiate itself and go beyond the regular and expected, which everyone else has.

True, there is nothing wrong with an idea that hasn't failed. But you have to consider what you've been missing out on, what you might not be reaching as a company because of an unwillingness to look at things in new ways.

I ended up buying a new elliptical because I wanted to start with a fresh canvas. I didn't want to change the style of workout; I love the motion and that it's low impact. I didn't take up marathon training or rock climbing. I simply approached something I'd always done with a fresh canvas and a new can of paint. And a shiny new elliptical.

And let me tell you, the workout is different. I walked into the kitchen after my first session on the machine, and my wife stared at me then asked if I was OK. I was drenched in sweat and felt both exhausted and invigorated all at once.

Whatever I thought working out on an elliptical was, this new machine has reconditioned my mindset of what it could be. Same workout, different approach. It isn't drastic, but it's new. I let myself be open to changing something that had been a habit for fourteen years, and I'm glad I did.

Your current set of ideas influence what you think you can achieve as a leader and as an organization. New ideas and approaches give you a perspective of what can be. Many times, when I work with new clients, they are in that limbo of balancing what they are and where they can go. They're asking themselves a critical question: What does our company have the potential to be?

Ask yourself that question right here, right now. Take a moment to really think about it. What does your company have the potential to be? Who do you, as an owner or leader within a family business, have the potential to be? Who do the people in your organization have the potential to be? What does your family have the potential to be, both in relationships with each other and in relationships within the business?

If you can answer those questions honestly, you are well on your way to preserving love, legacy and leadership.

AVOIDING COMPLACENCY

What was it that, after fourteen years, spurred me to consider a new way of doing things? It was a sense that things were getting boring and dull, that I was becoming complacent. I see the same "sixth sense" in leaders too. Often, they are in a routine, and they start to notice things are just too easy. They know they're not maximizing what they can do. That sixth sense says, "Hey, this is all fine and smooth right now, but it's just going too well. This is too simple. You need to shake things up." I call this purposeful disruption.

Perhaps you've felt that nagging sense for some time, or perhaps as you read these pages, that sneaking suspicion is beginning to make its way into your thinking.

Complacency can happen to anyone. Intelligent, ambitious people can be remarkably complacent in the face of needed change. Complacency can exist even when the profit and loss statements look good, even when things seem to be running well. It can sneak up on you, slowly and subtly, or it can appear one day and stare you down, eye to eye, a recognition that you're just not trying as hard anymore. Complacency isn't objective; it doesn't care whom it sets in on. Only those who take deliberate action to prevent complacency from taking over will be able to avoid it.

> **Complacency can happen to anyone. Intelligent, ambitious people can be remarkably complacent in the face of needed change.**

How does complacency develop? It's almost always a product of success or perceived success. It can persist long after the success has stopped. Perhaps most troubling, complacent people almost never recognize their mindset. When they begin to see numbers fall or issues increase within the company, they point elsewhere—the problem is always somewhere else. Only the most in-tune, aware and deliberate leaders are able to step back and recognize the grip of complacency on themselves and their organizations. These are the same people who have made a commitment to living and leading intentional lives and encouraging their companies to do the same.

Here's a problem, though. Oftentimes, it can be easy to myopically look at the profit and loss statements, shareholder returns and dividends. This is common in publicly held companies where these numbers are more likely to be the exclusive criteria for measuring performance. These organizations use quarterly earnings to measure their health and their success. I would contend that while numbers may be a measure of success for a given period of time, they are not a true indicator of an organization's health. In fact, they can become a rationale for complacency.

As we've explored, family businesses take a different view than of just the reported figures. Even if the numbers are steady, in-touch leaders begin to get that sixth sense that it's time to explore what can be. They know, or should know, what complacency means to their business. Leaders who are thriving want to push their organizations even further and maximize their performance and capacity—to *top* the top of their game.

How do you identify complacency in yourself or your leadership team? The best way is by examining what a person does, not what that person says. Behaviors matter more than words, although words can certainly be revealing. Here are some signs of complacency:

- Not actively looking for opportunities or risks facing the company, sales, profits and people

- Giving much more attention to what is happening internally rather than externally

- Tending to move at a pace of 30 miles per hour when 90 miles per hour is clearly needed to succeed

- Rarely initiating or truly leading

- Almost always doing what has worked in the past

- At a gut level, being content with the status quo

- Being irrationally afraid of the personal and corporate consequences of change

- Lacking a clearly defined and focused strategy of differentiation

- Failing to innovate, seek new ideas or adopt technology

- Not engaging one's team, employees or associates

If you recognize any of these qualities in yourself, don't worry. Just by acknowledging the possibility of complacency, you have taken an important step as a leader and put your organization's interests above your own. The next step is a little harder: leading intentionally. I'm going to ask you to push beyond what you know, what you've always done, to begin to thrive and advance both your leadership and organization.

You may honestly determine none of the signs apply to you, and if so, that's great. You are probably already thriving or at least moving in that direction. But chances are they apply to someone in your organization, so read on. I'll walk you through some concepts and advice to help shift to a place of truly maximizing the potential of your team.

GETTING CREATIVE

I used the examples of children and artists for a reason. Both are considered by our culture as creative beings. Leaders, though, are often considered more practical, less creative. Unless you are an inventor or what I call a "schizophrenic entrepreneur" (an endearing term, I assure you), you might not see your primary job as one of creativity.

Creativity, however, is not separate or distinct from practicality. A lot of times, people confuse the definition of creativity as being philosophical ahead of practical. Yet you can be deliberate and purposeful while still being creative. In fact, you have to be all three to thrive.

There is no better example of this than the retail industry. I spent twelve years in retail management during a time when that sphere was changing substantially. In the retail sector, things move quickly because consumer feedback is immediate; it happens at the point of sale. You can often look at a retail trend and see it moving downstream to manufacturing or industrial applications.

An example: bar-code scanners. Retail was the first industry to adopt this new technology in the 1970s. In 1972, Kroger piloted bar codes in a store in Cincinnati, Ohio. Soon after the widespread adoption of bar coding in retail, other industries followed suit. Hospitals began issuing bar-coded bracelets, the US Army used large bar codes to label boats, and research-

Creativity is not separate or distinct from practicality.

ers even used tiny bar codes to label bees in order to track their mating habits. Use of the bar code has extended especially into areas like shipping and tracking.[1] Imagine where retail giant Amazon would be without the bar code.

The bar code is a creative approach to real problems: inventory, labor costs and customer convenience. It was designed around information and efficiency. This creative solution certainly did not depart from practicality—it married the two.

Imagine if Kroger and other grocers had said, "Oh, well, this is how we've always done things. Let's just keep doing things the same way." It's possible another industry could have adopted the bar code, but it's unlikely there would have been the same widespread, uniform adoption of the UPC label that we have today. Yet despite such examples, leaders often shy away from creatively approaching challenges that face their businesses. Complacency says, "We know how to handle this." It can be agonizing for leaders to begin to think creatively.

Another challenge incoming leaders face in the family business is doing things their own way—differently than the previous generation. I've heard over and over again, "My dad did it this way," or "My mom always made this choice." Just because something worked for a past generation doesn't necessarily mean it's the best creative approach *now*.

The generational pressures are intense and full of opposing philosophies: the belief in what has been and the desire to change things. The inclination to follow the path of previous generations and the craving to carve out a new trail that is blazed by the current generation. The eagerness to use knowledge and experience of the past and the belief that many of those ideas seem somehow irrelevant or disconnected.

There are also recognitions: The realization that what used to be "advanced technology" has become an antiquated approach that puts the company behind the curve. The insight that previously accepted "absolute truths" from parents or mentors are challenged by current thoughts and beliefs. The awareness that while there are common values, leaders must do things in their own unique way and may even think differently.

These contradictions and recognitions don't represent either/or, right/wrong scenarios. Instead, they are simply differences to be understood and worked through.

When incoming leaders approach the business with fresh eyes, with an imaginative, creative perspective, there is a whole new set of colors with which to paint the canvas. Like a child with a new box of objects, these incoming leaders are able to see things in a completely novel way. But that's only if they are allowed to do so.

Let me say this again: Creativity does not depart from practicality. It is not an abstract idea. Leaders often think it is because they haven't seen it applied to the construct of their organizations. I urge you to take a different view. Be willing to look outside your industry. What is going on elsewhere that you might be able to apply to a problem or challenge you're facing now? How can you be more creative in coming up with solutions? If complacency has a grip on you, you must be intentional in exploring options outside of your past experiences and consider new ways of doing. Do so now with a planned approach, rather than being forced to later after a steady dip in profits or a failure in the company. It's difficult to be creative when facing such obstacles.

> **What makes you believe that what you've done to achieve success to this point will be what you need to achieve success in the future?**

Finally, I'll pose a question for you to deeply consider. Take time to contemplate your answer. Be honest with yourself. Write down your response if you feel compelled to do so. Or just pause for a few minutes to consider the question, fully and entirely.

What makes you believe that what you've done to achieve success to this point will be what you need to achieve success in the future?

You have to start thinking deliberately in order to start thinking creatively. In order to open your mind to broader thinking, you must actively consider what you need to change and evolve in your business and then build creatively around that. Do your due diligence in terms of creativity.

IT STARTS WITH YOU

There is a lot of buzz lately about "self-managed" or "leaderless" teams. In theory, it's great: Engage all people at all levels, encourage employees to take ownership, and focus on responsibility over tasks. Essentially, it's "giving people back their brains," as author Chuck Blakeman puts it in *Inc.*[2] In reality, leadership still matters. If you want that kind of open environment, it has to start at the top. It has to start with you.

If you've created a workplace where people are allowed to question old ideas in favor of new ones, creativity and innovation will become the norm rather than the exception. If not, people will remain silent because they know their ideas aren't going anywhere. It's up to you to create a company that encourages and welcomes a fresh canvas and new approach, where every individual feels encouraged to bring concepts forward.

This shift to maximizing, this evolution of your organization, begins with you. As an owner or leader, once you begin to shift, the organization will shift with you. It starts at the core—your behavior—and when you model behavior, people will change. This isn't about some sterile process or forms to fill out. It's about evolving behavior and awareness of yourself and others.

Your responsibility is simple: Foster a mentality of maximization. Promote an approach and environment in which challenging old notions is allowed and welcomed. Appreciate fresh perspectives. Do away with the sentiment that different should be attacked or dismissed simply because "it's not the way we do things around here." Give people permission to grow. Don't see different ideas as a questioning of your authority or competence but rather the development of people you are entrusting to lead, either now or in the future. You still retain decision-making; you get to ignore or adopt those fresh thoughts. That doesn't go away. But you must give people the power to think and bring those innovations forth.

History is a great teacher, but advancement rests on the student surpassing the master. As Seth Godin put it, "Leadership is the art of giving people a platform for spreading ideas that work."[3]

Ideas that work. Not ideas that worked in the past without consideration of the current needs of the company. Engagement isn't about age. It's about ideas that work: old, new or innovative; it doesn't matter. As a leader, you must create an environment in which people feel motivated and encouraged; have a platform for spreading ideas that work.

The first thing you need to do is get deliberate about considering a different approach. Think of a specific situation or challenge you're facing right now. Got it? Now, ask yourself these questions:

- Am I stuck approaching this situation the same way I've approached it in the past?

- When was the last time our leadership team really began to look differently at this situation?

- How can I consider this challenge with full creativity and recognition of a new idea and a new approach?

- Do we as a leadership team need to evolve our thinking in this area? Do I?

I'm not asking for a complete organizational overhaul. Simply answer these questions. And if you find that, yes, you need to explore your thinking a bit more, take the next step in doing so. Be deliberate and purposeful in exploring your options and the ways in which you could do things differently.

PEANUT BUTTER IDEAS

I love peanut butter. In fact, I would say it's my favorite food. So, when I was in New York City a while back, it's no wonder I had to visit a restaurant called Peanut Butter & Co. The eatery is distinguishable by its striped blue and white storefront and the giant peanut art that adorns the front windows. But it's better known for its takes on an old classic, the peanut butter and jelly sandwich.

You can order The Elvis, a grilled sandwich with peanut butter, honey and bacon. Or, if you're getting a special craving, try the Pregnant Lady®, a "strange sounding but great-tasting combination" of peanut butter and pickles. Spicy peanut butter and chicken, peanut butter cookies, peanut butter on celery with raisins— the options are nearly endless. Almost everything on the menu includes, you guessed it, peanut butter.

Peanut butter and jelly sandwiches aren't new. Most of us have been eating them since we were kids, and our parents ate them too. But the founder, Lee Zalben, saw an opportunity to refine and reinvent something that had been around for ages. Not only does he sell sandwiches in his shop, but his jarred peanut butter is sold in over ten thousand stores around the United States and in Canada, the United Kingdom, Japan and Hong Kong. He's known as the creator of gourmet peanut butter. People literally make pilgrimages to his sandwich shop.[4]

Zalben intuitively knew what many leaders fail to recognize: Refinement is a way of advancing and thriving.

Often, as I work with leaders, we find that old ideas need to be completely thrown out in favor of new ones. Leaders don't abandon history or culture but simply replace things that aren't working with things that are.

Other times, we realize that what is needed is a peanut butter idea. These family businesses don't need to completely throw out what they've done; they need to refine and recreate something that already exists to make it better, newer and more suited to what their company is, rather than what it was.

Business cannot be viewed as either/or. When I ask you to let go of what you think you know, I'm not asking you to do things *either* this way *or* that way. And I'm certainly not asking you to do a 180 and walk in the other direction. Instead, as a leader, letting go of what you

> **Refine and recreate something that already exists to make it better.**

think you know means recognizing complacency, being willing to truly look at people objectively, adopting a thriving mindset and, sometimes, thinking up peanut butter ideas. When you do all of these things, you can begin to thrive and advance on what you objectively know.

In what areas of your business can you take what you have— the peanut butter and jelly sandwich—and refine it or make it something else, using the same foundation? Or where can you completely abandon what you know as the peanut butter and jelly sandwich and reinvent something that is not only a variation but a brand new idea? A purposeful, creative approach will allow you to let go of what has been and consider what can be.

THRIVE AND MEASURE

Letting go of what you think you know comes, in part, through metrics. Not just measuring but looking at the results of those measurements with openness and a willingness to learn objectively.

In business, metrics are quantifiable. Measures define results. Output, production, customer numbers, expenses, profits—nearly everything can be measured. Unfortunately, the common perception is that processes involving people are not measurable.

People are too complex. They can't be measured. You can't know a person objectively.

Nope. That's wrong. You can.

Through an awareness process with leaders, I help them understand how this measurement works. I look at the total person and provide insights into how they do what they do, why they do what they do, the capacity they bring, and the skills and competencies they offer the company, team and position. My tools for this analysis include a series of assessments, in which I use five definable and practical dimensions to help understand each leader: assess, understand, align, advance and measure.

The five dimensions address key areas that help reveal a person's behaviors, motivators, capacities, competencies and emotional intelligence. They are part of establishing a common language for people to understand themselves, understand others (colleagues, family members and all relationships), and then apply what is known into a communication approach that values self and others. These assessments provide a unique perspective of looking at the individual as a total person.

If you go to the doctor for a persistent fever, and she only checks your blood pressure but doesn't look in your throat, ask questions about your health, or otherwise assess you in totality, it would be considered serious malpractice in the medical profession. Similarly, when providing true advice and guidance to a person or company, looking at just one aspect is negligent. The focus should be on total awareness of self, others and the organization.

After the assessments are complete, the leaders and I work through the results. The assessments aren't meant to say, "You're this way, and this is the only way you are." Instead, they begin to paint a picture of who the person is in terms of his behaviors and driving forces, capacity in terms of potential, and competency in terms of skills and emotional quotient. With individuals on a leadership team, for example, insights from the assessments begin to answer questions like: How will he handle a particular situation? Why does she view a problem or challenge a certain way? What is her potential? What might he have the demonstrated ability to do?

Now, a question for you: Have you ever painted a room? I bet you have. You probably went to a home improvement store to get paint, and when you looked at your choices, there were two options: standard or custom color.

In order to mix a custom color, you must start by selecting your color swatch. Then you get a neutral base and take the two to the mixing specialist. The paint specialist adds primary colors—red, yellow and blue—into the base in correct proportion to create the custom color. The mix must be exact. Just a small alteration of one of the primary colors can create a totally different color.

Like custom paint, people are a mix of a bunch of different motivators and behaviors, with each person a unique creation.

Yet people are beyond custom—they're distinctive. *You* are distinctive. *Your people* are distinctive. *Your family company* is distinctive. You must do the work of understanding yourself as a total and unique person and knowing others as total and unique people. When you do this, performance, turnover, selection, profitability, productivity, engagement, retention and too many other measures to name are positively impacted.

You don't have to separate people from objective measurement. You can really know and understand people by getting to the core of who they are and what drives them. No, you can't predict what people will do, but you can understand how they do things (behaviors) and why they do them (driving forces). You can't be 100 percent certain that a person will succeed in a position, but you can do due diligence in evaluating how a person is aligned to a position before she is ever hired or selected. Through a benchmarking process, you can specifically define accountabilities required for superior performance for the position and understand what alignment between the person and the position looks like in terms of behaviors, motivators, capacities, competencies and emotional intelligence. Then, you can compare a person to the positional requirements (the benchmarks), so you can begin to understand the gaps, development requirements, alignments or

> **You are distinctive. Your people are distinctive. Your family company is distinctive.**

lack thereof. That's how you measure a person against a position and performance.

I'm not going to tell you how to run your business; that's your area of expertise. My emphasis is in assessing, understanding and advising on the development of people and business processes that advance the performance of companies. And it doesn't start with the assessments—it starts with you. It starts with letting go of what you think you know. You must accept that even the keenest intuition can be flawed. In order to thrive and advance, you must objectively know your people and company.

DON'T JUST DO, THINK

We've talked a lot about letting go of what you think you know: about creativity, about ideation, about your company. We've also discussed measuring, both in terms of objectively measuring people and in asking yourself exploratory questions to get real about where you are and where you need to go as a leader. Yet all of this is for nothing if you don't make time for one thing: thinking.

I encourage and implore owners and leaders of family businesses to take time to think. Make purposeful time every single day to consider a problem deliberately. Be focused and allow the clarity to come.

I do this daily. Each morning, I get up at 4:30, drink my coffee, sit down to think, eat breakfast, and then exercise. During my thinking time, I focus on a problem, challenge or topic and give my mind over to considering the different ways I can approach a solution. Sometimes that time is spent creatively envisioning the possibilities of a specific idea. Other times, I am simply coming up with options. But I always invest the time.

I once worked with a leader who told me he didn't have time to spend "just" thinking every day. I challenged him to find time and make it a priority. He finally agreed that he could invest fifteen minutes a day but no more than that. That would be a challenge in and of itself. He made a commitment for a period of one week to spend fifteen minutes each morning thinking intentionally about a specific challenge.

By the end of the week, he was amazed. He found that he began his day with a level of clarity that enhanced both his creativity and productivity. He saw the ripple effect in meetings and interactions with his team and clients. Just the simple act of thinking radically transformed the way he leads.

Again, I implore you: Take time to think. Silence your phone and put it out of sight. Lock your door. Turn off your computer screen. Have out only a pen and paper, and access only your brain.

We work in such a hyper-speed world of business that thinking is easily dismissed in favor of doing. It's considered by many as unimportant in relating to others or evolving leadership. But if you don't make time to think, you will miss the opportunities that exist because you were doing or relating but not thinking.

I implore you: Take time to think.

Productivity is important; it's true. But thought is required at the level of a leader. No one else can think for you. Making time to engage your brain in a quiet, focused space is your greatest tool in advancing and thriving as a person and leader. Make a commitment here and now to spend deliberate time thinking each and every day. It will have the greatest impact on your leadership to date.

6

Developing Your Leadership Identity

There is a part of me that will always be defined by a certain incident I refer to as "toilet paper in Seattle." My life, my business, who I am has been forever affected by the white stuff you find in bathrooms.

About seventeen years ago, I was about to lead my first solo, full-day sales seminar in downtown Seattle. You met my mentor, Carlton, earlier—I was on the speaking circuit for his company. Who you haven't yet met is his then-fiancée, whom I'll call Angela, a highly compulsive, articulate and methodical perfectionist who worked as Carlton's assistant and event manager in charge of quality assurance. I liked the way she worked: everything in its place and structured. I knew she'd keep everything running smoothly.

The morning of the seminar, I felt confident and in control. But Angela kept asking me, "Are you ready?" I'd reply yes. She'd ask again, "Are you sure?"

Of course I was ready. I'd presented alongside Carlton multiple times. I knew the material inside and out. I could recite it in my sleep. Plus, I was a good speaker. I understood the transactional nature of communication—delivering good information to a crowd. I'd watched Carlton present more times than I could count, and I'd been to several other sales seminars.

Yet in all that time, in my preparation for this workshop, I hadn't thought about making the seminar my own. I figured I'd use Carlton's stories. I didn't need to think of stories from my own life and experience. I was good enough to use recycled material and make it interesting for the crowd.

The workshop started at 8:30 a.m. The room was packed, and as I made my way to the front, Angela gently pulled my arm, holding me back. She looked at me squarely. "Let's make sure everything goes the way it needs to go out there," she said. Her voice was light, but I could sense the undertone of "don't screw this up."

I approached the stage, said my hellos, and went through my welcome message. Then, I zoomed through the material. I delivered the content, but it lacked character, personality—it lacked *me*. I had just doled it out to the crowd, going through the content like it was a transaction. The first break was scheduled at 9:45; by 9:15, I had covered all of module one.

As I looked at the clock and realized I was running thirty minutes ahead of schedule, I began to feel the beads of sweat on my face. I had always perspired heavily, but this time was worse than I could ever recall. I looked at the audience and said simply, "Let's take a break." We agreed to meet back in fifteen minutes.

I rushed from the stage, knowing I'd tanked. Angela, as obsessive and orderly as she was, could also be tactful and compassionate. She looked at me and said, "Brent, what happened?"

I didn't know how to respond. I didn't know what had happened. I just knew I was stressed, hot and sweaty. I needed to cool down.

I made my way to the bathroom to wipe myself down with wet, cool paper towels. After running the dampened paper over my face, I instantly felt better. But when I went to get more towels to dry off with, they were out. I needed to get back in the room and start module two. I headed into a bathroom stall and grabbed a bunch of toilet paper to dry myself off, dabbing my face and neck, then made my way back into the room.

It was 9:30; lunch was at noon. As I worked my way to the front of the room, people began laughing and talking together. This was a disaster—one of the worst professional experiences of my life. I saw Angela take out her phone in the back of the room and step through a door and out of sight. I was certain she was about to call Carlton.

I began module two and, again, talked at 100 miles per hour. People were still laughing. I saw a few pointing in my direction. I thought, this is going poorly, sure—but this poorly? So badly that people are laughing? What a nightmare.

I finished module two and looked at my watch. 11:20. Forty minutes before I was supposed to finish.

"Let's break for lunch," I said, choking back nausea as sweat drenched my shirt. I saw Angela throw her hands up in question. "We'll take a long lunch today. See you at 1:00."

I made my way to the back of the room where Angela was waiting for me. I thought of the laughter in the room—had I really been that bad?

"Brent, have you looked at yourself?" Angela asked as soon as I was within hearing range.

"No, what do you mean?" I said.

"I've been trying to alert you the whole time. You didn't notice me pointing to my face? Go look in the bathroom mirror."

I made my way to the bathroom and discovered there was toilet paper all over my face. When I had wiped my sweat earlier, pieces of toilet paper had stuck to my skin, and it looked like I had toilet paper chicken pox. That's why everyone had been laughing.

As I stood in front of the mirror, brushing toilet paper off my face, I realized something. I had gone through all of the material. I'd covered what I had been taught to cover. But I hadn't made it mine. I hadn't done anything to give this seminar my voice, to put myself into it. I was talking at people, not to people or with people. I wasn't making it fun or interesting or inspiring. I was simply delivering information.

At that moment, I realized I needed some other avenue than just pure content. I needed to become more personable, not just a talking head. I needed to own it.

As 1:00 rolled around, I made my way up to the stage with a roll of toilet paper in my hand.

"Just so all of you can be like me," I began, "I brought a roll of toilet paper." The whole room cracked up. I went on. "I'm going to dole out sheets, and I'd like you all to wipe and blot your faces. That way, you can look like I did before lunch." The room erupted. As I listened to the laughter, I realized, if I put more *me* into this presentation, I get more time. If I get more time, I'll be OK. From that point on, I ditched all of Carlton's stories and shared examples of my own.

When I concluded, the entire room stood and clapped. We offered refunds to anyone who felt they hadn't gotten their money's worth, but no one took us up on it. They bought products and left happy and satisfied with the day's learning. I had pulled it off. But really, I had just pulled off finding my own voice.

Like the sweating version of myself seventeen years ago, maybe you are also at a place where you want to find your voice as a leader. I see this with generational transitions all the time, as the incoming generation struggles to establish their own leadership tradition. They want their voice, their values, their principles to be known. As an advisor, it's a privilege to help owners and leaders of family businesses find their purpose, voice and direction.

It all comes down to defining your leadership identity. Who are you as a leader? How are you different than the leaders who came before you or are leading alongside you? Are you properly aligned to your position within the company? What are the competencies critical for developing your own brand of leadership?

These questions serve as a starting point for exploring your identity, for finding your unique voice. The answers are the foundation by which you lead. They help you operate from a place of awareness.

You aren't your mom or dad, aunt or uncle. You're not the same as your brother, sister or cousin. For leaders who transcend into a mindset of thriving, there is almost always a cathartic moment of letting go of what was and adopting what is—*who you are*. When that awareness occurs, momentum is spurred. And while your own internal transition tran-

It all comes down to defining your leadership identity.

spires, so does a shift in your organization as you begin leading from a place of authenticity, from your own identity.

STOLEN IDENTITIES

We hear all the time about data breaches that lead to stolen identities. Companies exist solely to help people protect their identities. When a hacker steals your information, he's accessing a defined life: name, social security number, address, bank account information—the details that make up a person, at least on paper. He can then "be" that person as he goes on a shopping spree with someone else's money. At least until he's caught (which he probably will be).

But here's a thought. You can't steal a leadership identity. You must establish and develop one.

Finding your voice is really about finding your identity. It's answering a simple question: Who am I? In the family business structure, it's not uncommon for that question to go unanswered for years, even decades, as incoming leaders try to emulate the ones who came before them.

Who are you as a person? Who are you as a leader? It's a similar question asked two ways, looking for two like but different responses. If you don't understand yourself as a person, you're probably going to have a gap in your ability to sharpen and grow. As a leader, you must understand how you do things, why you do things, the capacity of your leadership, the competency of your leadership, and the emotional awareness or intelligence of your leadership, both intrapersonal and interpersonal.

If you don't know what you believe and don't consider who you are, how can you ever discover your identity? You have to determine what you believe so you can know who you are and define the identity of your leadership.

Imagine the completeness and security of knowing who you are. I'm not talking in psychology or therapy terms. It's knowing who you are when you walk in the door to your house, workplace, wherever it is you go. As a leader, this allows you to understand yourself professionally as an individual, so you can bring the greatest focus and clarity of leadership to your organization.

It's important, too, to understand that you can't separate the personal and the professional. You lead as a whole person, not part of a person; you lead the members of your team as whole people, not parts of people.

Decades ago, our culture left some room for compartmentalizing. I could be one person at home and one person at work. I'm not saying I could be two radically different people and lead effectively, but I could step inside my front door and leave my workday behind. If I wanted to, I could be the focused, driven leader at work and the easygoing, relaxed dad at home. There were no email or text messages to keep me tied to the office, and while cell phones were around, they certainly weren't used like they are today.

The evolution of our world—culture, technology, people—has changed to eliminate compartmentalization. This lack of separation makes understanding your identity all the more important, because you don't get to be two people. It's not you at work and you at home. You're a total person who exists between two spheres, more if you include social circles and other areas of your life. You have to confront the consistency of your leadership because phonies will be flushed out quicker today than ever before. Defining and knowing yourself as a leader will help you lead authentically and consistently.

We've explored the idea of personal assessments, and here's the main reason I utilize them: They help reveal strengths and limitations, and they assist leaders in creating a development picture while understanding leadership styles and approaches. And I'm not just talking about new leaders. There is no destination you can arrive at where you are suddenly given the key that opens the door to leadership completeness. The experienced leader who has defined and understands identity is fully aware of the need for conscious refinement to enhance leadership insight and skills. While new leaders may create a development picture to establish their identity and plan, seasoned leaders also need a plan for development that considers the refinements and evolutions necessary to maximize leadership. This is about awareness and understanding at every level. An identity cannot be determined accidentally.

> The experienced leader who has defined and understands identity is fully aware of the need for conscious refinement.

I look at defining identity in much the same way a company goes through brand development. When defining a brand, you look to what is and what the brand has the potential to be. Leadership is the same. You start with who you are, and by measuring your capacities, you look to who you can become. As Tom Rath, the author of *StrengthsFinder 2.0*, puts it, "You cannot be anything you want to be—but you can be a lot more of who you already are."[1]

The premise is completeness. I want you to be complete in your leadership identity, to understand your how and why. Then, I want you to begin to understand the how and why of others. That's where real leadership development begins.

LEADERS, DOERS AND ALIGNMENT

Central to leadership identity is understanding the difference between leaders and doers. Leaders influence people as a result of understanding themselves and others; doers are primarily focused on task and accomplishment within an organization. Getting these two roles confused can be extremely distressful to an organization. If you don't understand the unique capacities and competencies required for leadership, you may end up with doers in leadership roles, people who can accomplish tasks but have very little influence on people. This leaves the organization feeling uninspired and potentially somewhat stale. Unfortunately, I see a misalignment of leaders and doers in almost every organization I work with.

What makes this concept key to leadership identity is self-awareness. You might be at a place of determining which of the two you are: leader or doer. Perhaps you've been placed in a leadership capacity, but it hasn't felt like the right fit. Possibly, you're an owner who is trying to sort out how your son or daughter works into the transition of the company, and the idea that they might not be wired to lead is a reality you need to face. Maybe you're in an executive position trying to determine who on your team are the leaders and who are the doers—who will you train up to take over, and who will you develop to complete the necessary and important day-to-day tasks that keep the organization going?

I had a conversation recently with a company president as he was running through a series of names to consider who might be the best fit for ongoing development for his seat. There was an heir apparent, and the president recognized that he didn't have the intuitive sense of leadership. This individual was performing in his current role. The company was achieving record sales and profits, and yet the president of the company knew that this individual didn't possess the intuitive insight to make him a good fit for the seat. This was clearly a subjective factor, but the unique part was that this perspective was supported by his assessment.

The real problem in this circumstance wasn't experience in the current role or length of service with the company. The issue was that the heir apparent wasn't the right fit because he didn't know who he was as a leader and also because he hadn't recognized the gap between the reality of his leadership and what was needed. He was instead trying to get the position based on service and experience. This individual hadn't considered that his leadership identity was centered more in self than it was in others—and that was creating real heartburn for the current president because he knew he must look at other candidates internally.

This situation had led the president to what I call the "grasping-at-straws approach to succession and sustainability." Grasping at straws meant he had become primarily subjective in his considerations and was losing objectivity. In my conversation with the company president, I led him back to defining what the positional accountabilities for superior performance were for the position (benchmarking) and then comparing any and all candidates. Doing so helped him regain objectivity to pair with his subjective and intuitive understanding. When confusion exists because of subjectivity, I will always anchor my clients first in objectivity.

Subjectivity often pairs with assumption. Many owners and leaders assume that every family member is a leader. A father presumes his daughter will lead the organization. A nephew assumes that because his uncle was a great leader, he will be too. You may intend or desire for someone to be a leader, but if people do not yearn to influence others, then they are not aligned for leadership.

Other people may be aligned for leadership at one level but unsuited to lead at another level.

A common misconception is that you can't lead what you haven't done. Do you have to be the best doer to be a leader? No. What matters is understanding doing in a way that allows a person to be a highly effective leader. You have to understand doing; you have to understand people. Influence is the component of leadership that becomes more important than anything else.

I saw an apt illustration of this concept of leaders versus doers when a major fire broke out in the Phoenix area. The blaze was so large that it required around one hundred firefighters to battle the flames. Since the fire had compromised the structure of the building, firefighters had to be pulled out for safety, so they used a defensive strategy to save surrounding buildings.[2] Given the dangerous situation, they did what they needed to do, saving what they could, working together as a team to keep the fire from spreading. No injuries were reported, and while they lost one building, they saved countless others with their organized approach to the fire.

Now, imagine the scenario in a different way. Instead of one hundred firefighters working as one unit, there are one hundred firefighters fighting the flames with their own agendas. They are disorganized, scattered, running around with no direction or organization. There is no chief directing them as they attempt to save buildings and lives. Each firefighter is left to his own accord to handle things how he sees best. Different departments are showing up with hoses and water, aiming at wherever they

Many owners and leaders assume that every family member is a leader.

think makes the most sense, but their efforts aren't organized. How effectively do you think they would be able to put out that fire?

When you have one hundred firefighters responding to a two-alarm blaze, what becomes imperative is the objectivity of the plan to battle the flames. The efficiency of fighting the Phoenix fire came as a result of a collaborative, coordinated effort of multiple departments responding and fighting the fire. And at the head of the effort was the fire chief.

The chief, in this situation, was not a doer. He was a leader—the leader. He understood the act of doing, and he understood the people he was leading. But at that fire, like at every other fire he is in charge of, he was leading the team. He can't lead if he's out fighting the fire himself. Understanding the difference between leaders and doers, in his line of work, can mean the difference between life and death.

It might not feel as heavy a burden in their case, but family companies must operate much this way. There were one hundred firefighters on the scene that day; there may be ten family members leading an organization. In both situations, it's essential to have a clear understanding of the plan and an objective assessment of leaders and doers. The life or death of an organization depends on differentiating between the two.

As you search for your voice, as you begin to define your identity, part of that journey is understanding first where you align: leader or doer? There is nothing wrong with being a doer; it's just a different way of being. It's also true that doers can lead, just at another level. But if you determine that you are truly a high-level leader, there is responsibility in that role. And as a leader, you will inevitably have to determine where others fit, whether they are leaders or doers.

There must be doers. If you have doers in doing roles, that's great alignment. If you have leaders in doing roles or who are doing all the time and becoming frustrated, it's key to find outlets for them so they can become catalysts for growth in your organization.

I explained this concept to a client one day by taking him outside to look at plants growing on his property. There were two bushes side by side. One was struggling and one was flourishing. Near the bush that was flourishing, the surrounding vegetation was growing wildly, a rich, vibrant green. Near the bush that was struggling, the surrounding plants were wilting and turning brown, clearly at risk of dying off altogether.

Earlier that day, I'd noticed that the watering system wasn't working properly in the spot where the struggling bush was. Everything around this area was being watered, but these plants weren't. I'd also noticed that this company had stored its bags of fertilizer near the thriving bush. Bags are not airtight, and I could see the trail of fertilizer that had been washed down by rain and sprinklers. The line led straight to the flourishing plant.

If people are in the wrong positions in an organization—leaders in doer roles, doers in leader roles or leaders misaligned in a company—they will be like the struggling bush. Usually, owners and senior leaders look at people who aren't flourishing and wonder if they need to be uprooted altogether and replaced with individuals who will thrive. But often, people just need some attention. Like plants, they need water and food. With the proper positional alignment and developmental inputs that align with their identities, they'll flourish like crazy. It's rare that people need to be uprooted and tossed altogether; it's often a matter of transplanting them to positions that better align to what they need and giving them the nourishment to grow. In essence, it's about development ahead of destruction.

I've seen this misalignment happen too often in family companies. People end up in the wrong positions and don't get what they need to succeed. Often, this happens because family members are given opportunities in senior leadership positions that aren't aligned to their competencies and potential. The incoming leaders don't have a pull, a connection to their positions, other than "This is where I was told to go; this is what I was told I would do." The outgoing leadership picks new leaders from the heart instead of the head. They don't evaluate their children or other relatives objectively and fairly, and they don't allow them to have much, if any, say in where they are planted.

> Regardless of your position—owner or leader—I challenge you to strive for awareness.

I like to approach such situations with the three-thirds model of awareness. This model is most often used when considering external hires, but it can be used as an evaluation model for internal positions, as well. Think of it as a pie cut into three equal pieces. The first piece of the pie is subjective and deals with the experiential background of the person—the résumé or vitae factor.

The second piece of the pie is subjective and deals with cultural alignment, likability or the "get it" factor. It looks at whether the person intuitively fits the culture and "gets" the company or position and considers whether the team genuinely enjoys that person. People tell me all the time, "I don't have to like them. They just have to be able to do the job." But do people genuinely make significant investments in people they don't like? There is cognitive brain research that shows people move away from things they don't like more quickly than they move towards things they do like.[3]

The third piece of the pie is objective and deals with understanding the person through the use of assessment resources. The best decisions come when considering the totality of the pie, rather than just one piece. An assessment should not be the sole consideration, just as liking a person should not be the sole basis for making a decision. In a family business, you have to master all three thirds and so must others within your leadership team.

Regardless of your position—owner or leader—I challenge you to strive for awareness. Look objectively at people and positions. Find your own voice. Understand your identity. Understand the who, how and why of others. See where people aren't being nourished, or recognize if you're the one who is being deprived of food and water needed to grow. Only when you can begin to see the alignment discrepancies that exist will you be able to rectify the situation and flourish.

GROWING AS A LEADER

From 1977 to 1989, New York City was led by Mayor Ed Koch. An attorney, author and media icon, Koch was mayor during challenging times in NYC: a city near bankruptcy, rising homeless rates, and the AIDs crisis were just a few issues he faced.

Koch was best known for his brash, colorful personality. *The New York Times* wrote in an article shortly after his death in 2013: "Tall, squinty-eyed, baldish, with a nimbus of gray and a U-shape smile more satanic than cherubic, Mr. Koch told a story like a raconteur in a deli, kvetching and ah-hahing with the timing of a

Catskill comic. He loved to clown for photographers on the streets of New York, on a camel in Egypt or on a mechanized sweeper in China."[4] The media ate it up. Koch published seventeen books throughout the course of his life and even became a judge on the television show *The People's Court* from 1997 to 1999.

During his mayoral terms, Koch's atypical personality and often-swaying party affiliations meant he wasn't necessarily well liked in the world of politics. But he certainly had his supporters in the form of voters—enough to win the second and third mayoral elections by a landslide.[5] He was known by New Yorkers by his trademark, "How'm I doin'?" It was not out of the ordinary to find Koch standing at subway entrances, greeting passersby with this sincere question. He wanted to know how he was doing. He wanted to shake hands, look citizens in the eyes, and ask, "How'm I doin'?"

Koch fan or not, you have to admire the man's genuine, authentic approach to leadership. He welcomed—and wanted—all feedback. He was brutally honest and fearless. He was the opposite of complacent; he was a man as "all in" to improving himself as a person and a leader as he could be.

Growing as a leader begins by asking yourself these questions:

- How am I doing?

- How can I improve?

- When was the last time I thought of a truly provocative, intriguing idea?

- What am I doing now, and how could I maximize my performance?

- What could I be doing to maximize the performance of others?

Notice I don't use the word "better" in any of these questions. The focus isn't on what you can do better—it's on how you can maximize, how you can push yourself to become the greatest leader you can be. Be intentional, honest and self-reflective in considering these questions. They are the gateways to transformative thought.

The answers may come through private, focused thinking. They may be revealed through frank conversations. Honest feedback may arrive from customer surveys. Objective personal assessments, like the ones I use, can reveal where your strengths and limitations lie, while giving you a starting point to begin building on your strengths.

Brutal honesty. That's what you must be willing to hear. That's what you must be willing to confront. To grow, to advance, both now and in the future, you absolutely must be willing to hear the true and hard stuff. With that feedback, you can begin to modify decisions, alter interactions, change the way you strategize and plan. With the powerful tool of completely straightforward, honest feedback, you can start looking objectively at yourself and begin to plot out a plan for the future.

The leaders I work with, the ones who are all in and strive to transform their thinking and leadership, have a common trait: a desire to think. They want to work with someone who makes them think; they want to be challenged to think more and apply that thinking to their leadership and lives. (We'll look at the concept of thinking more in depth a little later in this chapter.)

It's been said that only the most confident leaders survive. This isn't a "fake it till you make it" idea. Leaders who want to grow themselves also want to grow the people around them. They purposefully provide the water and fertilizer. Leaders who aren't secure in themselves and their positions lack self-awareness, self-confidence, self-direction and role awareness—they're securely insecure. As a result, they push others down. They allow others to have a little influence but not too much.

Leaders who are confident in themselves know they are completely secure in who they are and the way they lead. They aren't perfect. Rather, they've taken the time to know themselves, build their strengths, neutralize their weaknesses, and become sharpened by others who push them to maximize their leadership. In turn, they do the same for their peers and teams, honing, pushing and helping others grow.

Growing as a leader starts with understanding yourself. When you understand yourself, you understand your role and direction— you stomp on the accelerator and power your organization faster in the direction of thriving. Great leaders start with themselves and branch out to others. They water and feed and nourish and help others thrive.

FOUR LEADERSHIP COMPETENCIES TO MASTER

Competency. We hear that word used in training seminars and business books, but it's rarely applied specifically to the dynamics of the family business. There are four key areas that every owner or leader in a family business must work towards mastering: clear thinking, leadership of self, leadership of others, and authenticity and transparency. Each contributes to the process of finding one's voice and identity. While it's true that these are really universal leadership sets, we will apply them specifically to the family business structure.

As my good friends and colleagues Ron Price and Randy Lisk put it in their book, *The Complete*

Growing as a leader starts with understanding yourself.

Leader, "The greatest leaders are always striving for more—always working to improve themselves and reach higher. They place importance not just on where they are but on where they have been and where they are going."[6] Wherever you are on the path towards developing these four competencies, there is always room to grow. There is always a way to improve. The first place to start: clear thinking.

CLEAR THINKING

Leaders go 100 miles per hour in a hundred different directions at a time. Even the most well-organized and intentional leader has a lot on her plate, dealing with many expected and unexpected things in the course of the day. That's a lot of doing.

By the nature of business, we are conditioned to do, do, do, do, do and then do some more. But clarity of thought requires stepping away from the doing, even if it's just for a short period. Earlier, I told the story of a leader who, on the outset, didn't think he had fifteen minutes to set aside each day. He became so inspired by the act of focused thinking that his fifteen minutes easily became forty-five minutes. He was able to process a problem and begin coming up with ideas for solutions simply because he thought intentionally. No distractions, no technology, just his brain and a pen and paper for company.

This leader discovered that once he began thinking about a problem, he suddenly had five or six ideas he wanted to talk to

> **Thinking must be related to doing or else you risk becoming a philosopher instead of a leader.**

his team about. He allowed himself time to come up with effective, creative solutions that he wouldn't have had the brain space to think of before.

For your fifteen minutes, think through an issue, and jot down every single thought your mind generates. Don't restrict yourself, don't correct spelling, don't try to figure out what anybody else wants—just let yourself go with a stream of consciousness. Write down what you discover.

The importance of clarity of thought is what it does for you and your business at the level of your leadership and influence. This is no more apparent than in the family structure, which requires a whole different set of relational dynamics on top of typical leadership. If you don't allow yourself the space to think quietly and uninterrupted, it can be difficult to hear yourself over the noise of emotion that can cloud decision-making in a family company.

Then, after you've thought, do. Thinking must be related to doing or else you risk becoming a philosopher instead of a leader. Not every idea will survive, but a couple will. You'll discover things about yourself and others in those thinking sessions that may have never been revealed without your intentional dedication to self-improvement.

To begin, you can focus your first thought session on this big-hitter question: How are you developing yourself mentally so you can see things more clearly?

Then, focus later sessions on other questions that push you to discover your company brand, as well as what brand strategist

Justin Foster refers to as your "leadership brand." As he puts it, this process of self-reflection and discovery helps you to "uncover this truth [your leadership brand] and align it with your career and/or business goals where it becomes the soil for growing your reputation, guiding your decisions and providing a constant source of self-expansion."[7] In separate thinking sessions, consider these questions:

- What's truly unique and interesting about my company?

- What's truly unique and interesting about me as a leader?

- In what ways have I positively disrupted my industry by amplifying our company brand with our customers?

- In what ways have I positively disrupted my company by amplifying my personal brand within our organization?

- What is the truth behind our company brand? What do we believe in?

- What is the truth behind my personal leadership brand? What do I believe in?

After you work through each of these questions, you must practically apply your discoveries. The best way to do that is to align your strategy to who you want to be as a leader or what you want your company to be in the marketplace. Many family companies don't focus on strategy because owners have determined consciously or subconsciously that they don't have time to think. But how can owners expect to advance their organization if the strategy doesn't exist, can't be communicated with others, and certainly can't be executed in actions? Delusion is a powerful adversary to clear thinking.

As my friend and author Steve Van Remortel—introduced earlier—puts it, "A recent *Forbes* study found that only 9 percent of companies tie their talent decisions to their strategy. Without strategy, your talent is not focused. Without talent, your strategy will not be executed. This is even more important for family businesses based on the sensitivities that come with talent and succession planning. It's simple: build a high performance team to Stop Selling Vanilla Ice Cream!"

Thinking time isn't "nice to have"; creating a strategy shouldn't happen "someday, when we have time." If you don't think, no one else will. If you don't apply that thinking to practicality through strategy, you'll continue doing what you've always done. Intentional thinking is your job, your duty, as a leader.

LEADERSHIP OF SELF

Too often in leadership, we focus outward. We look to what we are doing to inspire and influence others. Success is measured by how motivated and productive a team is or how smoothly a company is running. Financial reports are used to measure a leader's effectiveness.

But Plato had it right: "The first and best victory is to conquer self." Adopting a thriving mindset and leading your company to do the same begin inside. You must start with leading yourself, with being the kind of person you want others on your team to emulate. At the most practical level, leadership of self includes the following:

- Self-initiation: thinking, strategies, goals

- Self-observation: watching yourself, knowing yourself, understanding yourself

- Self-discipline: dedicating yourself to what may be difficult but is necessary

- Self-regulation: controlling yourself and your responses

- Self-expectation: defining what you want and need from yourself and clearly understanding what others want and need from you

- Self-criticism: reflecting objectively on yourself, so that whether you receive criticism from others or not, you are realistic about what's required to maximize yourself

Leadership of self is about the factors of consistency, continuity and constancy of self. Consistency in knowing what's expected of others and yourself and what holds your company together. Continuity in the unbroken and constant existence and operation of the business over time and throughout generations. Constancy in preserving the enduring and unchanging values of a family company with the willingness to consider and adopt new ideas to preserve and maximize.

> **Many times leaders will confront the symptoms, and what they really need to confront is the root cause.**

Leading yourself requires constantly asking the question of "what" followed by "why" as many times as it takes to get to the root cause of anything. Many times leaders will confront the symptoms, and what they really need to confront is the root cause. That requires the leadership of self.

It really comes down to personal accountability. Self-leadership asks the question: Am I being responsible for me? Great leaders demonstrate high levels of personal responsibility and accountability, day in and day out. They act with integrity not just in front of a room of employees but behind closed doors. They make the right decisions, even if they could make the wrong ones and not be found out. They see the worth in all people and treat them accordingly, even when no one else is watching.

It bears repeating: You cannot lead others until you lead yourself. Without effective self-leadership, you can't expect others to want to follow you as a leader. If you don't lead yourself effectively, you won't preserve the love, legacy and leadership of your company.

To help determine where you are in this process, ask yourself some questions:

- Do I know who I am?

- Do I understand my leadership identity?

- Do I have personal responsibility?

- Do I represent the values of the family? Of the organization?

- Is there consistency in what I say and do?

- Am I being accountable for me so I can earn the opportunity to be responsible and accountable for others?

Consistency of expectations, continuity of the company and constancy of values come from leading yourself. Accountability and responsibility are the basis of this competency. Developing as a leader truly flows outward, not inward.

LEADERSHIP OF OTHERS

His name was Sam. He was a tough-nosed, hard-working shop foreman at a construction equipment rental and sales company in Buffalo, New York. He was my boss, and he gave me the nickname "summer help." Sam provided what he referred to as his "daily dose of leadership." Every day on that summer job, Sam would call me to the middle of the shop floor to talk. He would then say, "If you're going to make something of yourself, then you have to make something of yourself. Here's your daily dose." What followed were practical words and purposeful thoughts from a person who was investing in me and the future of my leadership. Among the many practical things I learned that summer, three of Sam's daily tips stick in my head to this day: (1) Yelling may make you feel better, but it does nothing to inspire people; (2) know what you want to be known for; and (3) pay attention, and look for something to learn about leadership every time you interact with people.

Leadership of self leads directly into leadership of others. Understanding your leadership identity and effectively leading yourself provide the basis by which you can understand and communicate with others. This competency asks the question: Do I understand how others need me to lead them?

Understanding others as distinct is the key to effectively bringing them to their own awareness.

Too often, leaders answer this question off-the-cuff and fail to understand what makes each person they lead one of a kind. It's one thing to say people are unique. It's quite another to internalize that as a leader and actually lead and hold people accountable in a completely individualized manner. Understanding others as distinct is the key to effectively bringing them to their own awareness.

I encourage you to not shy away from the conversations and feedback that are essential for a person's growth. Instead, tackle them head-on by understanding those you lead as objectively as you can. Ask more questions and make less statements. In leading others, require that they first lead themselves. In managing others, require that they first manage themselves. And in asking people to think, make sure that you have first thought yourself.

Oftentimes, I see a battle between leadership by mandate and leadership by awareness. It's easiest to mandate what needs to happen. While I can get behind a direct style that focuses on the practicality of getting things done, I can't support a communication method that ignores the needs of people. You can't flat out disregard the ability to objectively understand others and expect to be effective. Great leadership takes into account who people are, their motivations, their drives and their alignment to their positions. It considers them in totality.

Assessing your leadership of others can begin through asking these questions:

- Am I willing to consider my strengths, limitations and needs for development?

- Am I willing to consider others' strengths, limitations and needs for development?

- What is my current influence as a leader, and in what areas is it diminishing, has it diminished or does it have the potential to diminish?

- When I look at others, do I see an opportunity to influence, or am I too focused on doing?

- When I consider myself, am I truly thinking in alignment with strategy in our business and taking the time to consider problems?

- In doing so, do I assess who might be the best person in the organization to solve those problems? Or do I simply respond intuitively based on what I think I know and assign people to those problems to just "get things done"?

With the last question, it's important to note that intuition is valuable. I don't want to dismiss the intuitive nature of leaders, because there are times and situations when it is not only useful but necessary. As a leader, you are likely where you are in part because of your intuitive nature. But not every issue has an instinctive answer—in fact, many require an objective approach. To lead effectively, you must be willing to take an approach based on objectivity when it's required.

An example I often come back to is hiring. In the family business structure, hiring can be a tricky thing. Often, you're looking at family members to fill key roles. You might be interviewing the nephew of a long-time employee for an entry-level job. Or perhaps you're assessing a daughter's effectiveness and whether she's capable of taking over the company someday. If you put too much subjective emphasis in the hiring process, you're missing out on a range of other important objective measures to align people with positions. In family companies, there's often a strong bias in favor of subjective factors such as likability, which impairs the company's ability to objectively consider the individual's fit in the organization. This is a failure to lead others effectively because it lets down not only the organization but the person who is being placed in the wrong position. Instead, look to knowing people objectively and aligning them properly.

As in hiring, leading others requires a willingness to step away from what you think you know. In leadership and in life, those who earn the true respect of others, who thrive as leaders and individuals, are the ones who look to themselves and others to advance and better understand their leadership.

AUTHENTICITY AND TRANSPARENCY

You've probably read or heard the words "authenticity" and "transparency" in the media recently. There is a lot of talk about those two words but little focus on what they actually mean. Being authentic and transparent means being straightforward and real. The terms cannot be separated from qualities like honesty, integrity and accountability.

Authentic and transparent leaders are *real*. They are willing to look at themselves and lead from the wholeness of who they are, both good and bad, positive and negative. They value their strengths and understand their limitations. They're not only willing to grow, they're willing to share their challenges and obstacles to help spur the growth of others. They acknowledge, "I don't know it all." They admit, "I don't understand it all." They are humble and recognize that vulnerability only increases their ability to influence others. They are not neutral fence-sitters; they are willing to be themselves, even when it might be controversial.

An authentic and transparent leader asks these questions:

- Am I willing to look at myself as thoroughly as I look at others?

- Do I speak to myself as critically as I speak to others?

- How am I balancing confidence and humility in the leadership of others?

- In what ways have I demonstrated that people can trust my leadership?

- Have I shared my own story of risk, success, failure and evolution so emerging leaders can learn and grow through understanding?

- When did I last state confidently "I don't know" as an answer?

- How well do I know myself?

- How well am I willing to let others get to know me?

In a family company, asking these questions is all the more important. You must strive to develop greater authenticity and transparency in every level of leadership. Begin by leading from a place of sincere vulnerability and awareness. Develop an understanding of what you're good at so

> **Some of the best conversations families have take place around the dinner table after the meal. Clearing the table signifies that while the meal is done, it doesn't mean that the conversation is over.**

you can lead from those strengths and successes while understanding your own shortcomings and failings. Be real and honest with yourself so you can be real and honest with those you lead.

One of the best ways to foster this authenticity is through "clearing the table." Some of the best conversations families have take place around the dinner table after the meal. Clearing the table signifies that while the meal is done, it doesn't mean that the conversation is over. This is why, when I work with clients, our opening session involves a round or U-shape table and a meal. This environment allows us to begin our work in a vulnerable and transparent way. Something about the table and food removes the pretense and replaces it with honest intentions.

By way of introduction, I give everyone at the table the opportunity to get to know me by asking any question they desire. I don't give a summary of my qualifications or overview of the process, though the owner always knows my intent. No script, no restrictions, no planned speech or introduction—just the unhindered opportunity to get to know me, and then I do the same with them.

The depth of what we learn around the table accelerates our relationship based on a simple formula: authenticity + transparency + insight = trust and credibility. We build the foundation for our work together with the entire team around the table. Let's eat!

MY OWN GROWTH

Early in my career, it was common to "lead" in a way that would never be supported today, at least I hope not. Yelling, screaming, jumping up and down, basically acting like an idiot—that was how many managers believed managing was done. You told people what to do, and if they didn't do it, you wrote them up. And frankly, that's how I was trained to manage people, even though it went against how I was raised to treat others.

The year was 1986. It was a Monday morning. I remember the details clearly because what occurred that day was a foundational moment in my life. In the span of less than an hour, the lessons of clear thinking, leadership of self, leadership of others, and transparency and authenticity became real, and I was confronted with the disconnect of my actions and words in a desire to climb the corporate ladder.

I was a manager working at a large retail organization, and every Monday morning, we had a manager's meeting. Remember, this was the 80s, so it was pre-cell phones, and the only method for communicating within a large location was through paging. Partway through the meeting, I heard the page: "Brent Patmos, please dial extension 477. Brent Patmos, please dial extension 477." Joann, a full-time lead associate who had been with the company for years, was paging me, even though she knew I was busy. I ignored the page—after all, I was in a manager's meeting. That was more important!

"Brent Patmos, please dial extension 477. Brent Patmos, please dial extension 477." It came again. And again. And again. I kept ignoring the page.

Finally, on the eighth page, I stormed out of the meeting, picked up a phone, and dialed Joann. I didn't give her a chance to speak.

"Joann, paging me eight times is not going to get me to respond," I said. "I'm in a manager's meeting. I will get with you when I'm done. Thank you." Click.

That was my really well-developed and aware response. Apparently, I thought I was above treating people like people. And that's how I was trained. Even though I was raised differently, even though I was taught never to treat others that way, I treated Joann disrespectfully.

The meeting ended, and I made my way downstairs to the first floor of the building. As I entered the retail floor, there was Joann, waiting for me. She stood right in the front area of the 235,000-square-foot building, with forty-two checkout lanes behind her and customers buzzing all around. She was staring right at me. She made a gesture at me, motioning me towards her. I went.

She gently grasped me by the arm then spoke. "I'm going to say this once and only once. If you ever do to me what you did to me moments ago, I will not only no longer support you, I will stop supporting all of what goes on in the department. It's not because I don't care about you, and it's not because I don't care about the department. It's because I will only page you if I need you because I know where you are every Monday morning. You are not the first manager to ever come through who believes he is going to conquer the world. So, unless you want to do that by yourself, I would recommend you learn the art of influence and understanding."

I looked at her and saw two things. First, genuine care for me as an individual and second, sincere interest in making me better as a person and specifically as a manager.

"Joann, I am sorry," I replied. "It will not happen again." And it didn't. Not to her, not to anyone.

I learned from Joann in that moment and in the years we worked together what it was to be consistent, accountable, reliable, honest and full of integrity. She was highly transparent and authentic. She was a leader by influence.

Why focus on developing key competencies? Because of people like Joann, people who care deeply about you and your organization. You owe it to them, to the legacy of your family company and to yourself to become the best version of you. Clear thinking is the foundation. Leadership of self sets the stage for more effective

Transparency and authenticity propel you to become straightforward and real, with honesty, integrity and accountability as core to your leadership.

leadership of others. And transparency and authenticity propel you to become straightforward and real, with honesty, integrity and accountability as core to your leadership. It's a critical mix, the foundation of four that transforms thinking, leadership, people and organizations.

7

Formulating Your Strategy

Since the first successful expedition to the summit of Mount Everest in 1953, approximately four thousand people have attempted the climb. Those who succeed get to stand on top of the tallest mountain in the world. At its peak, the giant measures in at more than twenty-nine thousand feet, allowing a person to look out over Tibet, India and Nepal. Climbing Everest has become a goal of people ranging from mountaineers to socialites—a challenge seen by many as the ultimate test of endurance.

Of course, climbing such a mountain can be deadly. As of this writing, approximately two hundred people have lost their lives in the attempt to reach the top.[1] In order to help avoid such a devastating outcome, guides and Sherpas need to create a strategy and execute that strategy flawlessly. They must have contingency plans to deal with the unexpected: avalanche, storms, falling debris, injury or any number of deadly threats along the way. Even a small misstep can result in disaster.

To prepare for the ascent, climbers are urged to start training up to three years in advance. They should take several courses in survival skills. They must have a carefully packed bag with the essentials needed to survive such a treacherous expedition. If they forget a harness or headlamp, they're at risk for more than a tough scolding. When they arrive at the mountain, they rely on their guide to have a plan—a safe, well-thought strategy—to get them from point A to point B and back.

If you don't value strategy, failure is predictable.

You are probably beginning to see the parallel I'm about to draw. You are the climber. You might even be the guide. Everest is your zenith, the place you want to achieve as a company. In order to get from point A to point B, you must think deliberately, develop a strategy, execute that plan and consistently measure your progress. Think, plan, do, measure.

Climbing Everest with just intuition as a guide would be a death wish. Experienced climbers who have summited several times might be able to get away with it for a while, but there would inevitably be something thrown in along the way to set them off course, headed for serious trouble. A strategy must be in place, flawlessly executed, to reach the zenith safely.

As an owner or leader in a family company, intuition cannot be your only guide for making decisions and growing your organization. You need a real strategy, not various transactional tactics being applied somewhat consistently. It's time to rethink your approach. Intuition and tactics are useful tools and certainly not to be dismissed. But if you want to move on from point A, you must have a strategy.

A strategy is a well-thought-out approach to get the organization from where it is to where the leadership wants it to go. It incorporates all elements of the company. In doing so, a strategy sets the foundation for an important perspective: It's about both the journey and the destination. The best leaders have a forward-thinking, readily adjusted strategy. Like a climber who sets her sights on a new mountain to conquer, such leaders are always looking for the next challenge. Once they reach point B, they dream up point C, a new zenith. And once that's reached—well, you get the idea.

Like a mountaineer, if you don't value strategy, failure is predictable. I have seen the best organizations, giants in their industries, get distracted for a minute and—boom—a sucker punch comes in and knocks the wind out of them. The ones with a strategy jump up and deal blows back, fighting their way back to success. The ones without a strategy keep getting the wind knocked out of them. They survive until they don't. A lack of a plan literally means shutting down the company for good or, sadly, selling a company the owner had hoped to keep in the family for generations to come because the company couldn't deal with all the problems they were facing.

Of course, there are times when the best strategy is, in fact, to sell the company. If owners understand this earlier on, they will have a much better strategy for selling. In family companies, knowing whether to stay in or get out may be the ultimate test of objectivity versus subjectivity. Sometimes owners must confront the reality of what *is* versus living with the delusion of what they wish *could be*.

As an owner or leader, you must be nimble and expedient in how your strategy is thought about, planned for, acted on and measured. In today's hypercompetitive marketplace, you can't fall in love with a method and abandon the adeptness to change or evolve when necessary. While a three- to five-year strategy is important and not to be overlooked, successful family companies are exceptional at designing and deploying twelve-, eighteen- and twenty-four-month strategies. They recognize and value the need to be swift. Like fighter planes, companies that are exceptional at definable strategy are often great at quick maneuvers to stay out of harm's way.

Unfortunately, family companies are more prone to lacking strategy for a couple of reasons. First, their ability to think longer term means they don't have to immediately adjust performance based on shareholder returns, as do publicly traded companies. Shareholders in family businesses are more patient with declining performance and will often rely on leaders' intuition to bring the company around. This can be a strength, but it can also be a weakness if there's too much tolerance for poor performance.

Additionally, many family organizations were built by entrepreneurs who relied on intuition, hard work and some measure of luck to succeed. As the company grew, these enterprisers became consumed in the day-to-day doing. Putting together a strategy is about stepping back from the doing to think clearly about the future. How can you understand your business if you've never thought intentionally about it? And how can you make progress if you don't take the time to articulate your thinking into something that provides a framework of action? That's the essence of strategy: a framework of action.

A leadership team I work with takes this task of thought related to strategy seriously. In the past, they claimed they were spending an adequate amount of time thinking daily about the business. However, they quickly realized adequate is different from effective and began to see thought as central to transforming their organization. I now meet with them quarterly to help them stay on track, maintain focus and keep strategy central to their leadership. There is connectivity between strategy, tactics to achieve strategy, and the execution that's required day-to-day. They are really thinking about their business. They are not relying solely on intuition to guide their decisions. And they are better leaders for it.

Company performance is also better for it. The organization is performing substantially beyond industry benchmarks and generously ahead of yearly goals.

Most of the companies I work with are trending positively, and a well-thought strategy helps them maximize. But there is another side to it. Unfortunately, too many organizations fly by the strategic seat of their pants for many years, until they inevitably begin to experience performance deficiency. Sales go down. Profits trend negatively. They keep trying the same techniques, the same intuitive approaches, but nothing works. They come to a moment of crisis because what they know to do intuitively isn't delivering. At that moment, what they need is strategic thought, strategic clarity. But what you'll often see leaders in these companies do instead is double down on a certain aspect of their business.

Here's how the dialogue goes: "We've just got to get more sales. We have to make more calls. We have to get out in the field more." That's not a strategy. Those are actions that can occur, tasks to do, tactics of accomplishment.

Instead, organizations should be answering these questions:

- How are we going to accomplish our objectives?

- What vertical are we going to emphasize?

- What particular product line are we going to go after, specifically?

- What is our most profitable product line? How do we know it's the most profitable?

- Who are our five most profitable customers and five least profitable customers? Why?

- What is an emerging trend we need to consider and discuss that is directly related to our business but hasn't necessarily been on our radar?

- In what area are we "behind the times" and would be better served in getting ourselves ahead of the curve?

- What internal process, system or area is most limiting the growth of our company? Why?

- What are our people talking about that we as leaders aren't talking about because it's viewed as a "hot potato" and continues to be ignored? Why?

On the last point, remember that "nothing" is not a viable answer. In the family company, just like in any company, there is often something that needs to be talked about that isn't being discussed because it's "political" or "off-limits" due to a leadership or organizational value. Talking about it doesn't mean it will change, but the leadership of a company should explore and examine without boundaries, so they can consider the predictable blind spots that accompany growth.

Leaders who focus on strategy answer these types of questions and more. They look to maximize return, minimize expenses and get people focused. They understand the relationship between thinking strategically, taking a deliberate approach and acting intuitively.

THE FORCE MULTIPLIER

The military uses the term "force multiplier" to describe a competitive differentiator. More specifically, a force multiplier is "a capability that, when added to and employed by a combat force, significantly increases the combat potential of that force and thus enhances the probability of successful mission accomplishment."[2] Applying that term to business, a force multiplier is something your company does so well that it creates a distinct competitive advantage in the marketplace. When executed by your "force," your people, it increases your potential and probability of thriving.

> In the family company there is often something that needs to be talked about that isn't being discussed because it's "political" or "off-limits."

What is it that your organization possesses that can be so relentlessly applied that it stands out as a competitive differentiator? Think about this question for a moment. The answer isn't a product. It's not something you can create, at least in a tangible form. If you manufacture sprinklers, it's not a specific sprinkler head, gear or material used in the manufacturing process. Those certainly can be differentiators, but they represent something different than what I am talking about here. What sets your company apart? In most family businesses, the natural answers are people and culture.

People and culture are the heart and lifeblood of your company, and no one—not your biggest competitor, not someone new to the marketplace—can duplicate them.

Let's take culture away from consideration for a moment and just consider people. Because, really, people are what make a culture go 'round, what allows an organization to establish a multiplying effect. Without people—passionate, inspired, driven, invested people—your organization will be like every other surviving company out there. As a leader, you can multiply the impact of your people by creating an environment where people think differently and clearly, have buy-in to what your company does, and come to work understanding the why of what they do. By creating a culture of valuing each person as distinct and important, people will give more of themselves to the company. And they'll encourage others to do the same.

Some organizations struggle to attract, engage and retain people. They are constantly looking for new talent to fill the gaps where old talent has jumped ship. Not so with organizations who have defined their force multiplier and built a strategy around it. When an organization has people or culture as a force multiplier, they rarely have to go find people. People come find them—good, devoted people of excellence who feel limited in their growth or development at their current places of employment. People who may be working at a publicly traded company but really enjoy the culture of a privately owned organization. Family companies have a much greater responsibility in choosing who joins their organization; the wrong fit could cause cultural erosion or unintentional disruption. The most self-aware leaders recognize and value the whole person, and that organizational tenet attracts talented people.

> Family companies have a much greater responsibility in choosing who joins their organization; the wrong fit could cause cultural erosion or unintentional disruption.

Organizations who really get this concept of the force multiplier are flying under the radar. Their competitors, try as they might, can't figure out what's making the difference. They'll look to products, price, customer service—every output that can be measured—to try to figure out how to compete. But the fact is that they can't. And unless competitors go through the same process, the same hard work, to understand what sets them apart and build a strategy around their differentiator, they will never truly compete.

Notice the phrase "build a strategy around their differentiator." Simply defining a force multiplier, while useful, is only a start. It then becomes central to a strategic plan. First, you must understand what your company does best so you can focus your energy there and enhance the probability of success. Defining your force multiplier with such clarity allows you to create a strategy around that distinct competitive advantage.

This clarity also allows you to create a common language everyone in your organization begins to identify with. This shared understanding and identification doesn't exist just at the senior levels of the organization. It flows down throughout the company and has a multiplying effect, catapulting the organization beyond others in their industry.

The real benefit of force multipliers is improving decision-making at every level. In fact, decision-making as a skill may well be a force multiplier in its own right, something that can't be duplicated by competitors. As Ron Price and Randy Lisk put it in *The Complete Leader*, "We all make innumerable decisions daily, most of which are made automatically. They seem obvious to us. Decisions range from simple (chocolate or strawberries for dessert) to complex (whether a company invests in a new facility).

Timelines and consequences of our decisions run from immediate to far in the future. Leadership is about taking an idea and making it happen through the efforts of the people involved."[3] Leaders who understand decision-making recognize that it's a mental process that results in a choice, and their choice leads to action. Consistency in decision-making and actions leads to decision-making as a competitive advantage.

How exactly does a force multiplier fit into your business strategy? It is the conduit to achieving a strategy. Having a well-defined strategic plan includes identifying the tactics, methods and people that need to be applied to problems and challenges. When you have a road map, when you understand your force multipliers, you can address challenges sooner and faster.

THE STARTING POINT

Years ago, I started noticing commercials on television advertising testosterone replacement therapies. The premise was simple: Apply the product to your underarm, and—voilà!—your hormone levels will be restored. Of course, every commercial followed with a quickly spoken list of warnings, but with such an exciting new option for men, who worried about such trivial things as side effects?

I knew men who bought into the hype. Not me. Instead of turning to medicine to counteract aging, I changed my lifestyle. I began exercising and eating better, dropped some weight, and began feeling years younger. I knew medication couldn't do that— at least not safely. Yet others insisted I should give it a try. "It's the greatest thing ever," a friend told me. Yeah, right, I thought. I'll stick with my regimen.

Not surprisingly, it wasn't long before this same friend had to stop using the hormone replacement because of an enlarged prostate. I felt terrible for him, but I wasn't surprised. There is no shortcut to good health. You can't reverse aging, but you can live a healthier lifestyle that makes you feel younger. It takes consistent hard work.

It's the same in business. I am sometimes confounded when people truly believe, "If I take the shortcut, it'll still get me where I want to go." It won't. I see leaders do this all the time. These aren't just leaders at failing companies; the shortcut mindset is often present in successful organizations, as well. Instead of taking the easy way, leaders must refresh the thriving mindset. Perhaps all they need to do is replace their elliptical—to look at their organizations with a fresh perspective, one that says, "I will do whatever it takes to thrive, because I can see where I have been, where I am, where I am not and where I want to go."

The starting point for developing the strategy of your family business is simple: Change or refresh your mindset. Strategic thinking—and a well-developed strategy—must become the cornerstone to your approach. It all comes back to a disciplined approach. You have to really buy in to the idea that a strategy is not a nice-to-have; it's a necessity. Follow the advice you give your team. How often have you said something like, "You can have all the ideas in the world, but if you don't develop a plan, they won't happen"? I bet you've counseled your employees on this idea dozens of times. Now, you must adopt the mindset you are likely trying to instill in others.

If you don't do it now when you have a choice, I can almost guarantee you will be forced to later. As an organization, you will reach a moment of crisis that flips you upside down, forcing you to shift the way you think—or perish. If you can alter your thinking when you are already at a zenith of performance or thriving, you get the opportunity to exponentially accelerate.

But maybe you're not there. You might be reading this book because you are barely surviving. That's OK. When you shift your mindset to one of thriving, consider your business carefully (think), create a strategy (plan), act on it (do), and continually assess your progress (measure), you will begin to see great changes in yourself, your people and your company. You will see the outcomes and ask yourself, why didn't I do this ten years ago? But at least you won't be looking back ten years from now, asking yourself, why didn't I do this twenty years ago?

> **Most of us move through life intuitively, making choices based on what seems the best option, until something shocks us into reality.**

It would have been nice if we all had the foresight to begin exercising regularly and eating a balanced diet in our teens. We'd all be better for it. But the reality is that most of us move through life intuitively, making choices based on what seems the best option, until something shocks us into reality. The change might come from a loved one dying or a compelling article on health. Or it might be forced by a diabetes diagnosis, high blood pressure or another health condition. Many of us won't make changes until something or someone gets through those thick heads of ours to convince us to change.

Don't be that person. Don't be that organization. Take the first step in your strategically planned future by shifting your mindset. Think. Plan. Do. Measure. That's the simplest yet hardest advice I can give you as a leader.

GETTING PRACTICAL

Starting your strategy can begin with two steps: asking yourself some questions and beginning to envision and create a strategy document or guide.

But before I lay out these starting guidelines, I want to be clear. I won't be giving you a seven-step guide to fix your business, nor will you find a complete approach in these pages. Every company is unique and must be approached as such. To assume otherwise would not only be arrogant but it would not allow for completeness of the approach, considering the entirety of a person and organization, which is the basis of my work as an advisor.

That said, there is a starting place for thought. Each person, no matter the level of leadership or company status, can begin to think more.

As you're considering the strategy of your business, ask yourself these questions:

- Where am I now? Start with an honest, thoughtful evaluation of your current state both individually and as an organization.

- Where do I want to go? Consider the possibilities. Think about your objectives.

- How will I get there? Think beyond tactics to instead consider what you see as the road map, the plan, towards achieving what is possible.

- How will I measure? Think about how you will assess your progress along the way.

- What are the force multipliers that will help us achieve company goals? This isn't about what you make or how you make it—it's people and culture. Think through what sets you apart from your competitors, an aspect of your company that is your competitive advantage that can't be duplicated.

- What competencies do I need to teach in my organization? Think of the ways you can grow yourself and those you lead.

- How can I define and understand people objectively? Be honest with yourself here. It's unlikely true objectivity currently exists. Consider how to make it a central part of your organization.

- What do I need to consider about evolving our company that is uniquely different than what it took to grow to this point? Really push yourself to consider how things have changed and how you and your business might need to transform to grow into the future.

- How can I best preserve love, legacy and leadership? Consider the one thing that would be essential to preservation in your company. Think through how your organization is doing in that area currently and what changes need to be made.

The heart of this process circles back to the first two questions. It really comes down to taking the time to sit down and think through where you are now and where you want to go. Intentional thought is the starting point of strategy. It's the place where change begins to happen. From there, action spurs growth, and the organization as a whole can begin to flourish.

As you consider your responses, you can start to create your strategy document. A strategy document is a single page that communicates the tenets of your strategy. It allows you to define what you want to work on and creates accountability for your initiatives. It also creates the organizational yardstick by which you can measure your progression.

Since there is no one quick-fix pill for organizational success, you need to sit down with someone skilled in strategy to create a strategic approach that is specific and unique to your company. But first, you can begin to consider the components of a strategy in preparation for a bigger discussion and strategy initiative within your organization. Creating a strategy document will help you in this process, as it typically brings objectivity by assessing specifics related to both you and others, including non-family members. It should be related to the following areas:

- Behaviors: how you best communicate and interact with those around you and how others best communicate and interact with you. This allows you to maximize the conversation through increased effectiveness.

- Driving forces: what moves you to action, why you make your decisions, and how you frame your perspectives; what moves others in your company to action, why they make their decisions, and how they frame their perspectives. This further advances understanding of the value people bring to their roles or positions.

- Acumen capacity: how you analyze and interpret your experience. Your acumen, insight, and depth of perception or discernment are directly related to understanding your level of performance and the performance of others.

- Competence: the overview and ranking of twenty-five key business competencies that define your major strengths and the strengths of others. Understanding your well-developed capabilities will reveal where you are naturally most effective in focusing your effort, emphasis and time.

- Stress: the aspects of your organization or leadership that are leading to the greatest distress. Finding ways to manage stress isn't about making huge changes or rethinking career ambitions but rather about focusing on the things that are within your control.

- Emotional awareness: the ability to sense, understand, and effectively apply the power and acumen of emotions to facilitate higher levels of collaboration and productivity. The outcome and impact of highly aware leaders is reflected in the results they achieve through people.

Keep in mind that these areas deal with part of your strategic approach but certainly not all of it. And know, too, that you should be approaching this practically—don't let this process get so extreme that you need a psychologist to sort through it all. These are just the first steps: thinking and beginning to envision your strategy. At this point, you're not focusing on the tasks and tools. You're focusing on generating a greater sense of awareness—a theme you are familiar with by this point in the book.

When I need my roof replaced, I hire the best roofing company to skillfully redo my roof. I'm looking for quality. I'm not concerned about price alone, and I won't ask the roofers what kinds of hammers and nails they use. Similarly, as you begin

You can have brilliant breakthroughs in thought and all the intent in the world, but you must, must, must follow with action.

these preliminary strategic steps, you need to focus on the bigger picture, creating a vision of the future (the new roof) and understanding how to best reach that future (with the best possible roofing team).

Considering behaviors, driving forces, acumen capacity, competence, stress and emotional awareness expands your perspective to see what you could be doing that you aren't doing now. But this process is just a start. You can have brilliant breakthroughs in thought and all the intent in the world, but you must, must, must follow with action. You must move forward. You must think. You must plan. You must do. You must measure.

A strategy is only as good as its execution. It is the plan that sets the stage for change. You start by thinking; you change by doing.

REACHING YOUR ZENITH

To people like me who aren't mountaineers, it can be hard to understand why a person would want to climb Everest. Setting aside the fact that the climb itself is physically difficult, death or permanent disability is a very real risk that every climber takes on. Yet while I will likely never climb any of the Seven Summits, I can appreciate the draw to challenge and desire to achieve a goal. Some people feel a call to conquer, to push themselves even when they don't have to. That is me in the area of learning and application in business trends and concepts that directly impact my clients. I may not understand why climbers want to summit Everest just like they may not understand why I would want to read business books. That is my pleasure reading. And yet, uniquely, we both understand the challenge that we want to confront and achieve.

As one resource site for climbers puts it, "Everest offers the lucky rest of us [who survive] a tremendous insight in ourselves and the human kind; as we and our fellow climbers are tried in brutally exposing situations . . . Everest shows you the grace of great dreams, fears overcome and, sometimes, triumph following the most desperate of outlooks."[4] Consider this quote thoughtfully, as it applies to family companies, as well.

As both climbers and business leaders know, achieving a goal is about more than luck. It's about getting intentional, creating a strategy, preparing for the journey, and flawlessly executing the plan. When slipups occur, adjustments are made. Along the way, leaders and mountaineers savor the journey. They overcome the challenges and approach the future wiser with a more objective perspective. They apply a disciplined approach and hard work to reach their zenith. And when they conquer one goal, they look to the next goal, the next zenith.

Companies, like climbers, don't always live on mountaintops. All organizations dip to the valleys of performance. The goal is to maximize the mountaintop moments.

Try not to make decisions in the valley, where all you can see is the disappointment of a decision gone badly. Instead, strive to make decisions at the mountaintop, at the zenith, where you have a broad view that sweeps across every possibility. The valley is where decisions of desperation are made. The zenith offers decisions of choice.

I have an immense respect for the leaders I work with. Their commitment to discipline and evolving past what they think they know sets them apart not just in their fields or among family companies. It sets them apart in business itself because they are striving for greatness. They have a drive, an intense desire, an inner fire that pushes them to distinction. They understand and implement a strategy because that's what they need to do to achieve their next zenith. And you know what? They'll reach that zenith. And they'll continue to set new goals and climb new heights, always focusing forward, always seeing the promise of the future.

8

Where You've Been and Where You're Going

Years ago, I began working with four brothers, all scientists. These brothers were deeply passionate about their work within the family company, a scientific lab started by their mom and dad. If you were to talk with the two surviving brothers today, you would gain a deep sense of what value, work ethic and integrity mean to their family—a cultural foundation set by their parents. It's not uncommon for one of the brothers to get tears in his eyes when describing the culture established by his parents. Since the lab's early years, its culture has carried to the community and lasts today, attached securely to the family name and especially the two living brothers who are continuing the legacy of their family.

Yet as unbreakable as the culture seemed when we started working together, it was not enough to carry the organization entirely. There weren't major problems in the company; balance sheets were fine, and profits were holding steady. But the company was beginning to miss certain things, and their approach to people and processes was self-limiting. They lacked objective awareness and didn't understand the complexity people brought to positions or why people-position alignment was so critical. They were operating from a place of intuition rather than a viewpoint of clarity.

These brothers had made choices largely on the foundation of culture and the belief that their cultural heritage would carry them through. They believed in the profession of laboratory science and the trust that had been established in their customer base.

Then, they experienced the marketplace: at times ruthlessly unrelenting and mercilessly brutal. As they lived through those bumps, they had to let go a bit. Not let go of culture—they still clutched tightly to it. Not let go of their belief in the profession— their trust in science only deepened. But they had to let go of what they thought they knew so they could objectively know what was going on in their business, why the bumps at times felt like land mines. They had to recognize that belief in culture, in the company, in the people was not enough. These scientists had to recognize that their penchant for objectivity could extend into the people sphere too.

Their CEO was instrumental in this shift of applying objectivity to all aspects of the business. A non-family member, he wasn't an operator, he was a strategist. The owners had to get rid of the idea that he could do it all. And he was the first to raise his hand and say he needed help. He could strategize, but his area of expertise wasn't in running the day-to-day operations, even though he was—and is—exceptional in doing the tasks and functions of scientific research.

The two brothers and CEO had to come to a place of understanding, a point where they could begin to establish a new picture of what the company could be. They needed to create new positions within the organization, ones that would support maximizing.

This was a hard shift for them because they had to get rid of the "old way" of doing things. In many ways, everything looked great, which made it hard to change. But if you were to peel back the layer of happy people who loved where they worked, you would have begun to see a lack of clarity about who was going to help advance the company into the future. Basically, they loved each other just a little too much. There were talented people misaligned to their positions. And all of this was directly connected to having no relevant strategy for the current marketplace. They lacked a defined plan of action connecting who they were, why they were there, where they were going, and how they were going to get there.

The owners also had to shift the way they worked. As scientists, they were thinkers and plodders, moving slowly to make changes. They needed to put urgency behind their actions in order to propel themselves forward in a marketplace that certainly wasn't going to wait for them to catch up. I have to give them tremendous credit because, while the process was at times uncomfortable, they worked with me in lockstep at every point along the way. To see them now fulfilling their strategy and executing on their own is a source of pride for me as an advisor.

One of the brothers recently "retired" from his positional role, and the other is redefining his role, which is the correct thing to do for the future of the business. That's because the legacy of the company, while still being carried forward by them at one level, is now being carried forward by leaders who have been with the company a long time and aren't related by name but are certainly family. These leaders represent multiple generations with an awareness of what it will take to preserve this family company into the future.

That company has now catapulted forward to grow their effectiveness and profits. The brothers are no longer merely surviving on culture. They are drawing on their force multiplier, their culture, to thrive and continue the legacy built by their mom and dad. They are the definition of shifting to a thriving mindset.

When the company began the advisory process, I remember sitting around a table in their boardroom. As I looked at each leader in that room, I realized the organization was one of the most functionally dysfunctional I've seen. Here's why: They were all seated at the table pretending everything was wonderful, sweet and hunky-dory. But the CEO spoke up. He was no longer comfortable with functional dysfunction. He looked me in the eyes and told me he didn't know how to grow the company on his own, and he needed me to help them. And finally, he said that the company was going to move forward, and he would not be the person in the way—he would confront his own leadership completeness so everyone else could do the same.

Change started with the CEO. In your organization, it starts with you.

BEYOND LEGACY INTO SUSTAINABILITY

I learned my lesson after the U of M china incident, and my wife and I now possess four sets of china owned at one time by men and women in our families. These dishes have been used at family gatherings for over one hundred years. They are more than porcelain; they are legacy. Their use represents a connection between the generations, a bridge between the past and present.

Passing down heirlooms like dishes or safes used to be the norm. Things were made well, with care and quality, and families cherished those pieces as part of the family heritage. When the next generation received such priceless artifacts, it was seen as an honor.

In many ways, my generation represents a mental stopping point for the legacy of passing down family heirlooms like china. Everything since my parents' generation has become disposable and much less formal in its approach. Today, passing things down is an oddity in a culture that is often defined by its speed, expediency, expendability and disposable nature. We use then we throw away (or recycle). There is no legacy in transferring a paper cup and straw; they don't stand the test of time. But there is something that flows rich and deep in the undercurrent of my family in passing down items like china, in transferring ownership of a safe, in the lessons and stories I have learned from my father, mother, grandparents and other relatives. Those are legacy.

When I think of legacy, I'm often reminded of my grandfather on my mom's side. He worked for the postal service and school district. Above all else, he was a tinkerer and what he called a gardener—I call it small-scale farming. Grandpa would go to the "garden" to think, and I would join him. This was my "oak tree," though it was actually a willow with a tire swing, with acres and acres of grass and plantings surrounding it.

My grandfather liked to share common sense and wisdom during these garden talks. I can remember one Sunday when I went to my grandparents' house after church. I was so excited to get on the tractor that I ran in the house, changed my clothes, and went to the barn and fired it up. I was off and running when, the next thing I saw, my grandfather was sprinting towards me, telling me to shut it down.

"If your grandmother catches you out here cutting the grass on a Sunday, it will be your hide and mine at the same time," he told me. "I appreciate your enthusiasm and hard work, but we have to respect that Grandma sees Sunday as our rest day. Now park the tractor, get in the house and let's eat." This is where I learned the value of relationship between respect, rest and hard work. Interestingly enough, Grandma was perfectly fine having me clear the table and sweep the floor after every meal when we were at their house. Even on a Sunday.

Both sets of grandparents, while uniquely different, taught me the same values in differing ways. They taught me to think, and yet they did it differently. Both of my grandmothers were hard-working, determined women, as well. One taught me to darn socks using a light bulb, and the other taught me how to iron, pick currants and set up a fruit cellar. I didn't recognize legacy then; I was too young and unaware. But now I clearly understand the legacy of what my parents and grandparents taught me because I can remember vividly how each experience has impacted and shaped my life.

Transitioning ownership of a family company is about more than signing over the building, just like my china is about more than the dishes themselves, and just as the time with my grandfather under the willow was about more than the details of every conversation. For owners and leaders in family companies, transferring the values, beliefs and sound structure of the company through multiple generations is the ultimate mark of success. It's not about money; it's about family.

Legacy refers to something that has happened in the past. For many leaders, legacy is embodied in the culture built through generations of dedicated business ownership, devotion to the field, and a deep care for their people. Legacy matters. Legacy is about continuing to cherish those values that are the essence of the business and not deviating from those principles for the mere sake of opportunity. Legacy guides leaders to make decisions from a place of integrity, not just because that's what the leaders want to do but because it's what is right for the organization and its people.

Yet for all its merits, it's important to remember one thing: Legacy is an *outcome* of sustainability.

To have lasting impact, a family business must incorporate legacy into new and innovative ideas and strategies. As an owner or leader, you cannot depend on legacy to carry you through the next decade, let alone the next generation. Continuity of culture joined

> **For owners and leaders in family companies, transferring the values, beliefs and sound structure of the company through multiple generations is the ultimate mark of success.**

by clarity, objectivity and strategy is what sets apart the 3 percent that thrive into the fourth generation from those who disintegrate after the second.

Looking beyond legacy doesn't mean ignoring it. Rather, legacy becomes a facet of success, a feature that helps distinguish your organization from others. Legacy is an outcome of the hard work you put in every day to create and maintain a sustainable culture, so your organization can stand the test of time.

Sustainability is built by reinvesting in people. There is no other way. I don't mean investment in terms of capital; I mean providing knowledge and growth opportunities to individuals who have invested their lives into your family's company to help continue your legacy. Yes, strategy is critical, and we've explored that at length. But people make the strategy happen. They make legacies last.

You've heard about sustainability in terms of the environment. Sustainability is about existing "in productive harmony . . . fulfilling the social, economic and other requirements of present and future generations."[1] It's about permanence, focusing on the greater good.

Why don't more businesses adopt an attitude of sustainability with their leaders and people at all levels in their organizations?

Millennials today average around just three years of tenure within an organization, according to a report from the Bureau of Labor Statistics. Older generations tend to stay for more than a decade.[2] What is making young people switch companies, even switch careers entirely? Why aren't they staying at companies longer? The cost of replacing people is high, with estimates for senior leadership and executive replacement as much as 213 percent of the person's annual salary.[3] Leaders need to find a way to retain and develop talent.

A sustainable organization creates opportunity for people inside its walls. Its leaders create experiences for its people, the experiences they crave. They do so, in part, by creating as much excitement about linear movement as upward movement.

In a traditional organization, reward is hierarchical gain. You climb up the ladder. Linear movement—a structure more common in family companies—offers more varied rewards. And since this structure is less established, you as a leader get to define what those rewards are.

Linear movement fosters sustainability because it creates new experiences and opportunities for people. Individuals are given different responsibilities and accountabilities, without creating unnecessary bureaucracy or burden on the organization through cost or positions. To make this structure work, leaders must position linear movement as being as beneficial to the individual and organization as hierarchical movement—because it is. Linear movement gives people the opportunity to stay engaged and

A sustainable organization creates opportunity for people inside its walls.

interested in their work, while rounding out their competencies and capacity within the company. They move on to other experiences, have new exposures, and do so while contributing to the sustainability of the organization simply by their devoted tenure and dedication. As an outgrowth, legacy continues.

When I talk about looking beyond legacy, I don't mean losing sight of your family's and company's values and roots. I am saying that legacy continues only when organizations boldly focus on sustainability that is centered on growing and retaining talented, dedicated and driven people.

After all, how can a legacy continue if the organization is no longer around? A focus on sustainability—on thinking, planning, doing and measuring with people as a central focus—is what makes organizations last.

WHERE CAN YOU GO?

Where am I now and where do I want to go? Those self-reflective questions are two of the most powerful starting points for change. They open up possibility, the chance for a more purposeful future, one that has you tackling yet another evolution of your business. The questions spur thought and encourage the mind to think a bit differently than it has in the past—to push the boundaries of what *is* to consider what *could be*.

As you think about your life, leadership and organization, let me lay out some possibilities for you. We have spent pages focusing on key areas of growth and awareness and considering where that awareness can take your organization. Your future can open up in a way it never has before. It can include:

Defining a leadership identity. As an individual, understanding and defining your identity as a leader means being able to look in the mirror every day and know who you are, what you should be doing, why you should be doing it, and how you can do it. It means having clarity around yourself and your role in the company. When leaders in an organization define roles and align people to those roles, they allow individuals to maximize their leadership identities and achieve the highest levels of clarity, effectiveness and performance.

Shifting to a mindset that preserves love, legacy and leadership. You get to make the choice whether to flourish. The decision to prosper is the recognition that you are expanding deliberately, purposefully and strategically in your business, understanding all the things that go on: hopes, aspirations, fears, concerns and questions. If you remain deliberate in thinking, planning, doing and measuring, greater returns aren't only possible, they're predictable.

Blending awareness and decision-making. Too many decisions are one-dimensional. This approach is self-limiting, because myopic decisions create myopic results. If you expand your awareness to what you actually know, you can become less one-dimensional in your thinking, while broadening your view and making more informed and effective decisions.

Closing the subjectivity/objectivity gap. The intuitive, subjective, experience-based dynamics of business—and often the day-to-day routines—can become limiting. If you can push yourself to look at things objectively, while still valuing intuition, you will make better choices that spur growth.

Proactively assessing, understanding and aligning. Good people in the wrong positions don't maximize results. It's the same with good ideas not implemented. You have the ability to look at every area of your business objectively and really understand it for what it is—not protect or abandon it unnecessarily—and align a strategy to improve where improvement is needed. I have watched this happen again and again.

Overcoming bias towards family relationships. In a family business, emotion is intimately tied to nearly every aspect of an organization, and that can negatively impact making sound business decisions. If you define love of family in the way most people do, you will have the tough conversations. You can learn to do so in a way that values and respects the person but does not place the relationship ahead of the objective decision required for the business.

Understanding your contribution to complete leadership. Advancing as a leader means being willing to look at yourself and others, evaluate challenges, and consider strategies for growth. It's about approaching the totality of a person.

Understanding the completeness of leadership allows you to shift from being a doer to an influencer—and aids in helping upcoming leaders do the same.

Making decisions that produce actual results. You can make decisions that are not based on fads or trends, not just words for the sake of words. By using the think-plan-do-measure method, you set your organization and yourself up to succeed, not just today but through the next year, next decade and next generation.

These are the possibilities—the probabilities—of what can occur when you begin to change as a leader. Leaders must endorse and support true organizational evolution. It begins with you. It starts with your leadership team. The change will then encompass and seep into every facet of your organization, propelling the company you care so deeply about into a future of prosperity that will continue well beyond your leadership tenure.

THE NEVER-ENDING JOURNEY

I named my company Perpetual Development to describe the journey of leadership. Perpetual means never ending. The journey of family companies is just that, a never-ending journey. Unless, of course, that business stops growing, halts developing and ceases considering ways to advance purposeful growth.

Do you have a desire for perpetual growth, success and development of people? Great family companies consistently answer yes.

Never-ending growth. What does that mean? An organization that has the capacity, competence, culture, clarity, communication, collaboration, cooperation and respect for never-ending growth is an organization that has the ability to perform like the biggest wave. A wave is a perpetual flow of water, crashing into the shore, going out again and starting all over. In the surfing world, the biggest wave is called the maverick.

The maverick is the wave everybody wants to ride. It is of epic proportion. Every organization has the opportunity to become the maverick, to become the largest wave. And it doesn't have to be in terms of size or volume; it can be in effectiveness. In the privately held world, being the best and preeminent company in a specific space is often the maverick goal.

Many times, organizations are so hypercritical of themselves that they forget their objective is never-ending growth—the journey and evolution of their organization, people and performance. And sometimes they feel they have become buried by that wave, that biggest of waves. It pushes them down, crushes them. They can't get out from under it; they can't breathe.

> **The change will propel the company you care so deeply about into a future of prosperity that will continue well beyond your leadership tenure.**

What's the most important thing for a surfer to remember if a wave crashes down on her? Don't panic. Tumble, toss, get turned about but don't panic. The minute a surfer panics, she's going to make things worse, and it's not going to end well.

So, what do surfers learn? Be disciplined; don't panic. What do the leaders I work with learn? Be disciplined; don't panic. Possess urgency, awareness and understanding of what you've got to do to handle the tumultuous times that will present themselves in business.

But also recognize that the same water that pummeled you is the water that is going to take you in. It's the water you're going to ride back out. If you will accept the process for what it is, you have the opportunity to achieve never-ending development and never-ending growth. You can guide the perpetual development of yourself and those you lead.

About the Author

Brent Patmos is a business advisor and the founder of Perpetual Development Inc. He has spent more than thirty years working with leaders in privately held and family-owned companies to create sustainable business growth and cultural continuity by providing transition clarity, developing leadership competencies and advancing strategic thinking. Brent lives in the Phoenix area with his wife, Trudy, where they spend most of their time outdoors, whether it's in their backyard with their four grown children or exploring trails with their dog.

Notes

CHAPTER| 1

1. "Family Business Facts," *Conway Center for Family Business,* http://www.familybusinesscenter.com/resources/ family-business-facts/.

2. Ibid.

3. Lauren Weber, "Today's Personality Tests Raise the Bar for Job Seekers," *The Wall Street Journal,* last modified April 14, 2015, http://www.wsj.com/articles/a-personality-test-could-stand-in-the-way-of-your-next-job-1429065001.

CHAPTER| 2

1. Tara Parker-Pope, "Is Marriage Good for Your Health?," The New York Times Magazine, April 14, 2010, http://www.ny-times.com/2010/04/18/magazine/18marriage-t.html?_r=0.

2. Rawn Shah, "Working with Five Generations in the Workplace," *Forbes,* April 20, 2011, http://www.forbes.com/ sites/rawnshah/2011/04/20/working-with-five-generations-in-the-workplace/.

3. "The Millennial Generation Research Review," *U.S. Chamber of Commerce Foundation*, 2015, http://www.uschamberfoundation.org/millennial-generation-research-review.

4. Father Vincent Serpa, O. P., "Who Said, 'Love the Sinner, Hate the Sin'?," *Catholic Answers*, http://www.catholic.com/quickquestions/who-said-love-the-sinner-hate-the-sin.

5. Diane Brady, "Jack Welch: An Oral History," *Bloomberg Business*, August 28, 2012, http://www.bloomberg.com/bw/articles/2012-08-09/jack-welch-an-oral-history.

6. George Stalk Jr. and Henry Foley, "Avoid the Traps That Can Destroy Family Businesses," *Harvard Business Review*, January–February 2012, https://hbr.org/2012/01/avoid-the-traps-that-can-destroy-family-businesses.

7. Patricia Cohen, "One Company's New Minimum Wage: $70,000 a Year," *The New York Times*, April 13, 2015, http://www.nytimes.com/2015/04/14/business/owner-of-gravity-payments-a-credit-card-processor-is-setting-a-new-minimum-wage-70000-a-year.html.

8. Geoff Colvin, "For GE, Breaking Up Is Hard to Do," *Fortune*, August 21, 2015, http://fortune.com/2015/08/21/general-electric-end-of-conglomerates/.

9. Aaron De Smet, Mark Loch, and Bill Schaninger, "The Link between Profits and Organizational Performance," *The McKinsey Quarterly*, no. 3 (2007), https://solutions.mckinsey.com/catalog/media/TheLinkBetweenProfitsAndOrganizationalPerformance.pdf.

10. "Wilma Rudolph," *Olympic.org*, http://www.olympic.org/wilma-rudolph.

CHAPTER| 3

1. "World's Greatest Leaders," *Fortune,* March 2015, http://fortune.com/worlds-greatest-leaders/.

2. "Learn More about Our Company," *The J.M. Smucker Company*, http://www.jmsmucker.com/.

3. "Our Culture," *The J.M. Smucker Company*, http://www.jmsmucker.com/smuckers-corporate/company-values.

4. "Frequently Asked Questions," *S. C. Johnson*, http://www.scjohnson.com/en/company/faqs.aspx.

5. "About Us," *Dutch Bros. Coffee*, http://dutchbros.com/AboutUs/.

6. "The Future of Design, Shopping, Education, Robotics, and More," *Bloomberg Business*, last modified June 8, 2015, http://www.bloomberg.com/news/articles/2015-05-07/the-future-of-design-shopping-education-robotics-and-more.

CHAPTER| 4

1. *Merriam-Webster Online*, s.v. "culture," http://www.merriam-webster.com/dictionary/culture.

CHAPTER| 5

1. Tony Seideman, "Barcodes Sweep the World," *Barcoding Incorporated*, http://www.barcoding.com/information/barcode_history.shtml.

2. Chuck Blakeman, "Why Self-Managed Teams Are the Future of Business," *Inc.*, November 25, 2014, http://www.inc.com/chuck-blakeman/why-self-managed-teams-are-the-future-of-business.html.

3. Ekaterina Walter, "50 Heavyweight Leadership Quotes," *Forbes*, September 30, 2013, http://www.forbes.com/sites/ekaterinawalter/2013/09/30/50-heavyweight-leadership-quotes/.

4. "About Us," *Peanut Butter & Co.*, http://ilovepeanutbutter.com/about.

CHAPTER| 6

1. Tom Rath, "The Fallacy behind the American Dream," *Gallup*, excerpted from *StrengthsFinder 2.0*, February 8, 2007, http://www.gallup.com/businessjournal/26278/fallacy-behind-american-dream.aspx.

2. "Dozens of Firefighters Battle Blaze at Phoenix Warehouse," *AZFamily.com*, last modified April 11, 2015, http://www.azfamily.com/story/28779610/dozens-of-firefighters-battle-blaze-at-phoenix-warehouse.

3. Dr. Ron Bonnstetter, "The Hidden Brain and Its Decisions" (TTI SI 2015 International Conference, Fort McDowell Resort, Fort McDowell, AZ, January 10–12, 2015).

4. Robert D. McFadden, "Edward I. Koch, a Mayor as Brash, Shrewd and Colorful as the City He Led, Dies at 88," *The New York Times*, February 1, 2013, http://www.nytimes.com/2013/02/02/nyregion/edward-i-koch-ex-mayor-of-new-york-dies.html.

5. "Ed Koch Biography," *Bio*, http://www.biography.com/people/ed-koch-9367324.

6. Ron Price and Randy Lisk, *The Complete Leader* (Boise, ID: Aloha Publishing, 2014), 15.

7. "Methodology," *Foster Thinking*, http://www.fosterthinking.com/resume.

CHAPTER| 7

1. "Mount Everest by the Numbers: Deaths, Cost to Climb, and More Mountain Records," *The Daily Beast*, May 21, 2012, http://www.thedailybeast.com/articles/2012/05/21/mount-everest-by-the-numbers-deaths-cost-to-climb-more-mountain-records.html.

2. *Dictionary of Military and Associated Terms*, s.v. "force multiplier," http://www.thefreedictionary.com/force+multiplier.

3. Price and Lisk, *The Complete Leader*, 93.

4. "The Dream," MountEverest.net, http://www.mounteverest.net/expguide/dream.htm.

CHAPTER| 8

1. "Learn about Sustainability," *United States Environmental Protection Agency*, last modified September 21, 2015, http://www2.epa.gov/sustainability/learn-about-sustainability.

2. "Employee Tenure in 2014," *Bureau of Labor Statistics*, September 18, 2014, http://www.bls.gov/news.release/pdf/tenure.pdf.

3. Heather Boushey and Sarah Jane Glynn, "There Are Significant Business Costs to Replacing Employees," *Center for American Progress*, November 16, 2012, https://www.americanprogress.org/issues/labor/report/2012/11/16/44464/there-are-significant-business-costs-to-replacing-employees/.

Appreciation and Acknowledgement

> "Life is not tried, it is merely survived,
> when you're standing outside the fire."
>
> – Garth Brooks

This is my appreciation and acknowledgement for the irrational and outrageous generosity of the people and leaders who have contributed so significantly to my awareness, my understanding and my development. Please view this book as a return on your investment. Thank you to each of you.

Trudy (My shotgun rider, right where you belong)

Magoo and Magee

Navy Man and Subaru

Mom, Dad and Mom Vera

Alyssa (I have changed the picture)

Amy H.

DIL, Switzerland and Yogi

Stacy (Using your gift as the connector of dots)

Tim (I never heard of Hutch before you)

Isaac (You make a difference through people)

Mark S. (It all began on a day in September)

Mark S. (Despite being an OSU Fan)

The people of FM (The BEST)

Allen (My brother...)

Ron (TCL)

Jamie E. (Quietly inspiring "Brentisms" for ten years)

SVR (YTM)

Ryan (YTM)

The men and women of the CHRC (Service Above Self)

Stewart (My first solo in Florida)

Tricia (My sister from another mother)

John K. (Your leadership and mentorship remain with me today)

Adrienne (Strength and determination)

Carlton (Mother Goose, this is roving hen. Fulfilling our purpose.)

Angelina, Kim, Rachel and Robin (Each of you define professionalism and mastery of your craft)

James 1:4 (Clarity above all else)

Going **BEYOND THE NAME** doesn't happen overnight; it's a process. It starts with purposeful and intentional thought and leadership that your people value.

For additional resources, downloads, chapter videos, podcasts, and #thoughtstarters visit:

GoBeyondtheName.com

Sign up for weekly insights on family business, purposeful growth, and objective leadership at

brentpatmos.com

Join the conversation on social.

Follow **@BrentPatmos** and use

#BeyondtheName on Twitter.

CPSIA information can be obtained at www.ICGtesting.com
Printed in the USA
BVOW08*1953170516

448443BV00002B/2/P